Praise for *The Bu*

T0017585

The missing ingredient in ministry is often business acumen. *The Business of Ministry* brings together mission, heart, practical business concepts, and God's leading. Pastor Jeff Simmons also shares personal stories where opportunities were filtered through ministry and business principles. This book is like having a trusted friend kindly and gently mentor you. I highly recommend this for anyone in ministry at any level.

PAUL SCHMITZ, Executive Director and Cofounder, ShowerUp

There are so many transferrable principles from business to ministry. After serving for years in the church and nonprofit space, I can attest that this book will help your organization make a greater impact for the kingdom of God. I can't wait for you to read it and apply.

CONNIA NELSON, Senior Vice President & CHRO, Lifeway Christian Resources

Every ministry leader should read this book. It doesn't matter whether you are just beginning your ministry work or are a seasoned ministry veteran, there is something in *The Business of Ministry* for you. Page after page, I felt God encouraging me where I needed it, and reminding me to include Him in the areas that I have been trying to do things on my own.

STEVE NORRIS, President, 4:13 Strong

The Business of Ministry is a must-read for every pastor and ministry leader. As someone who has worked on the business side of church for over thirty-two years, I'm firmly convinced that God is not only interested in this aspect of ministry, but I believe He is greatly glorified when the local church is operating effectively and efficiently. Jeff Simmons is a faithful pastor who not only understands these realities but has effectively implemented principles that work. You will find this book to be compelling and inspiring, yet also accessible and practical. You will glean something that will immediately strengthen you and your ministry.

DENNIS BLYTHE, Executive Pastor, The Church at Brook Hills

What if every church and nonprofit reached their full potential? Can you imagine what a difference there would be in the world today? This is a book that can help your church or ministry grow and make a difference for the glory of God today.

MARY KATHARINE HUNT, CEO of Justice & Mercy International

Ministries are best when they are effective, focused, efficient, and organized. Jeff Simmons understands these principles and applies them in his life, ministry, and message. This book equips those in ministry desiring to be great stewards of the resources entrusted to them.

RICK WELDAY, Business Executive with Fortune 50 company

My friend, Jeff Simmons, has always possessed a unique blend of talent. He has the compassion of a pastor, but also the acumen of a CEO. This new book is a culmination of these two streams of giftedness. This is a must-read for anyone considering "ministry" but also a must-read for anyone wanting to be a faithful steward of God's resources. May our work for Jesus increase tenfold in impact on the world He died to save!

WAYNE WILLIAMS, Lead Pastor, Renew Church

After decades of leading ministries and nonprofits, Jeff shares practical principles to the inspiring stories that will assist ministry leaders in making decisions to help them lead their organizations more effectively. You will find this book hard to put down. I am excited to hear of the numerous ministries that will benefit by putting these principles into action. You will want to read this book with a pen/highlighter in your hand because it is jam-packed with takeaways for your ministry.

KEN THOMAS, President of Connect Ministries

After serving for over fifty years in the faith-based nonprofit space, I can attest that this book will help your organization make a greater impact for the kingdom of God. I have watched Jeff and his church and nonprofit practice these principles. This book is not a book filled with theory; rather, it's a book of proven practical sound advice. Because ministry is business and business is ministry. I can't wait for you to read it and apply it.

TOM ATEMA, Cofounder of Heart for Lebanon; Founder & CEO of Vertical Horizons Group

How to Maximize God's
Resources for Kingdom Impact

THE
BUSINESS
OF
MINISTRY

JEFF SIMMONS

MOODY PUBLISHERS
CHICAGO

Unless otherwise noted, all Scripture quotations are taken from the Holman Christian Standard Bible®, Copyright © 1999, 2000, 2002, 2003, 2009 by Holman Bible Publishers. Used by permission. Holman Christian Standard Bible®, Holman CSB®, and HCSB® are federally registered trademarks of Holman Bible Publishers.

Scripture quotations marked (NIV) are taken from the Holy Bible, New International Version®, NIV®. Copyright © 1973, 1978, 1984, 2011 by Biblica, Inc.™ Used by permission of Zondervan. All rights reserved worldwide. www.zondervan.com The "NIV" and "New International Version" are trademarks registered in the United States Patent and Trademark Office by Biblica, Inc.™

All emphasis in Scripture has been added.

Published in association with the literary agency of Steve Laube Agency.

Edited by Avrie Roberts
Interior design: Ragont Design
Cover design: Erik M. Peterson
Cover graphic of bar graph copyright © 2023 by kirasolly/Adobe Stock (170624355). All rights reserved.

Library of Congress Cataloging-in-Publication Data

Names: Simmons, Jeff (Pastor) author.
Title: The business of ministry : how to maximize God's resources for
    kingdom impact / Jeff Simmons.
Description: Chicago : Moody Publishers, [2024] | Includes bibliographical
    references. | Summary: "Ministries need help and guidance to become
    effective and wise stewards of the resources entrusted to us by God.
    When pastors and nonprofit leaders are good at the business side of
    their ministry, more people can be supported. This book helps us
    maximize our resources for greater kingdom impact"-- Provided by
    publisher.
Identifiers: LCCN 2023035259 (print) | LCCN 2023035260 (ebook) | ISBN
    9780802431677 | ISBN 9780802473196 (ebook)
Subjects: LCSH: Church management. | Church personnel management. |
    Christian leadership. | Business--Religious aspects--Christianity. |
    BISAC: RELIGION / Christian Ministry / Pastoral Resources | RELIGION /
    Christian Church / Growth
Classification: LCC BV652 .S525 2024 (print) | LCC BV652 (ebook) | DDC
    254--dc23/eng/20230914
LC record available at https://lccn.loc.gov/2023035259
LC ebook record available at https://lccn.loc.gov/2023035260

Originally delivered by fleets of horse-drawn wagons, the affordable paperbacks from D. L. Moody's publishing house resourced the church and served everyday people. Now, after more than 125 years of publishing and ministry, Moody Publishers' mission remains the same—even if our delivery systems have changed a bit. For more information on other books (and resources) created from a biblical perspective, go to www.moodypublishers.com or write to:

Moody Publishers
820 N. LaSalle Boulevard
Chicago, IL 60610

1 3 5 7 9 10 8 6 4 2

Printed in the United States of America

This book is dedicated to the One who has called us to steward His church and work in our day and generation. May He find us faithful.

CONTENTS

INTRODUCTION

God works through people. To live your life for the glory of God is the greatest joy and journey ever. You can be a businessperson, a teacher, a stay-at-home parent, or someone called into full-time vocational ministry. This is true for all of us. It is not always easy to live your life fully committed to Christ and His calling, but we are redeemed in order to be conformed to the image of Jesus and to live on mission with God.

God, in His sovereignty, has chosen you. God does not need any of us, but He invites us and allows us to be involved in what He is doing in the world. And God has given you opportunities, gifts, and a unique sphere of influence. Our call is to be the best we can be for His glory in the short time we have on this earth, to steward what He has entrusted to us for maximum kingdom impact. This is how God chooses to change the world for His glory—through each of us, His children.

This book is not an exhaustive work, or an academic textbook. It is a book to equip those serving in ministry to do the work God has called us to do. I pray this book will help you. It is written after years in ministry and with many business principles that we can apply to maximize the impact for God's kingdom. I believe this book will help you. It is written from a heart of prayer and encouragement for you. I am a servant of the Lord alongside you. Let's continue to grow, learn, and give our best to build His kingdom and transform lives—and, I pray, our world—for His glory.

If you are a senior leader in a ministry, serving in a church, or working in business, then this book is for you. We should all desire to get better at what God has called us to do. Whether we lead a small group, serve at a church with children or students, serve on a committee at church, or even lead a growing ministry, there is always something we can learn from the business world. We all want to do ministry more efficiently and effectively for the glory of God.

This begins with asking God for wisdom. When Solomon became king, God gave him the opportunity to ask for anything he wanted. Imagine what you would ask for. Solomon didn't ask God for long life, death to his enemies, or even wealth. With his one wish, Solomon asked God for wisdom—wisdom to lead God's people since it was such an enormous responsibility. Because Solomon asked for wisdom and not these other things, God answered his request and Solomon became the wisest man who has ever lived. He also became the wealthiest man of his time and one of the greatest builders and businessmen as well.

There is a difference between wisdom and knowledge. There is so much knowledge out there today. You can Google anything or "ask Siri." But, with access to all that knowledge, the world is not becoming a better place. We need wisdom. Wisdom is the practical application of knowledge. It's where the real power of godly leadership comes from. Wisdom comes through our relationship with God. Sometimes we only listen to other people's opinions, but we all need godly wisdom in our life. This comes through prayer, reading God's Word, and hearing from other godly leaders. We all need wisdom to lead the church, nonprofit, or ministry area God has entrusted to us. Listen to what God is saying to you about how you lead. Trust and follow Him. Wisdom is where great leaders receive their power and influence.

Wisdom matters for all of us. Ask God how He wants you to apply what you will take away from this book. Business principles can help you do even greater work for the kingdom. Consider this—it was Christians who started the first hospitals, schools, hospices, soup kitchens, orphanages, and more. The called-out ones, the risk takers, the "businessmen and -women" of the church, the teachers, the pastors, the leaders who recognized that God had uniquely gifted them not just to make money for themselves and build their own kingdom that wouldn't last, but to build God's kingdom and make an eternal impact.

There are many transferable principles in business that can help churches and nonprofits do greater ministry for the kingdom. For instance, businesses do market research before they launch a product to determine the need and receptivity of the people they are trying to reach. Businesses have target markets because they realize they can't do everything, so they want to invest in what is most effective. Businesses do mid-year and annual performance evaluations to help ensure their employees, along with the business, are still headed in the right direction. Businesses also set one-year, three-year, and five-year goals to keep them moving forward.

Churches and nonprofits in the past have intentionally or unintentionally applied business principles like these to maximize kingdom impact, and the results have changed the world. The early church cared for the sick, shared the gospel, educated the next generation, and ministered to the underserved in their communities. God has always used His people to accomplish His will in this world. Through Christians living out their calling, our world is forever changed.

God has called us to impact the world for Christ Jesus. This is humbling and yet invigorating. There is no greater joy in all the world than using your gifts for the glory of God, and you feel like this is why you were created. We should give our best for His glory.

This is our time to learn, grow, and be our best—to make disciples and grow Christ-centered ministries to impact the world for Christ. Growing up, when we would go camping, my dad would always tell us, "Leave it better than you found it." This is our call today. To leave this world, God's church, your family, and your ministry better than you found it. To pass on to the next generation the love, joy, and grace we have received in Christ.

The business of ministry is stewarding and maximizing the assets

God has entrusted to you for impacting people's lives in the name of Jesus. God has given us so much, especially if you are reading this in the United States. We have access to greater resources than ever in history, and we must learn to steward all of it well. As followers of Christ, this is our time not to retreat but to engage. We have been given so much, and how we handle what has been given is important to God, ourselves, our families, our communities, and our world today, as well as to the next generations.

Some have said that Christianity is one generation away from extinction. You read the statistics today about the rise of the "nones" (people having no faith and no belief in God), and it seems like Christianity is in trouble. And I say, "Not on our watch." We must learn to live our personal calling and do ministry better. We must be strong and courageous. To lay down our lives and small dreams. William Carey said, "Expect great things from God. Attempt great things for God."[1] This is our time, so let's learn, grow, and give our best for the glory of our great God. He is calling you. How will you respond?

Part 1

Purpose

Becoming the Best Stewards of God's Resources

The purpose of ministry is to build up the body of Christ and to serve others. In churches, nonprofits, and other ministry organizations, the needs of others are met through the gifts and actions of staff and volunteers in the organization. This is the call of Jesus to all His followers. Ministry is not just for paid "ministers and priests," but for every person who is a follower of Christ.

The purpose of business is to provide the economic exchange of goods and services. Businesses receive financial compensation for the goods and services they provide, and the money they receive is used to support the life needs of the business owner and employees, and it can also be used to benefit others.

Not everyone is called to go into full-time vocational ministry, but if you are a Christ follower you have a call to ministry. We need more Christian men and women in business. We need followers of Jesus working and serving in businesses throughout our country and world. This is where godly leaders become salt and light. This is where the gospel spreads. We also need Christian business leaders living out their calling by serving in their local churches and nonprofits. This is where the kingdom of God grows.

Chapter 1

JOB VS. CALLING

When I was in college, my dream was to be a Christian businessman like my dad. I don't think ministry and business are mutually exclusive; in fact, our God is the One who created us to accomplish goals and
tasks. There is much that Christians can learn from business leaders, and
vice versa. And, as we do, we grow and help each other become better
equipped to fulfill our calling.

By God's grace, I came to know the Lord early in my life. Growing up
I always thought I would be a Christian businessman like my father and
many of the people I looked up to at church. I graduated with a degree in
business—a BA in finance and marketing. I worked hard during school
to prepare, secured internships, and studied in one of the best business
schools around. I wanted to have a great job, make money, teach Sunday
school for students, serve on committees, go on mission trips, and tithe
generously to my local church to build God's church and His kingdom. I
am so thankful for all the Christian businessmen and -women out there
who live out their faith in Jesus. However—God had another plan for
my life.

After graduation, I had the opportunity to interview for a big job in a
major US city. The job was in their management training program, and it

had a great starting salary with international travel. It was what I always thought I wanted. The company flew me to their headquarters and put me up in a nice hotel. I spent a full day in interviews that all went well. I thought this was it. Until . . .

Until that night. As I lay in the hotel room, I couldn't sleep. I tossed and turned. I didn't feel at peace and felt like God was trying to speak to me. Have you ever been there? You know something is not right, but you don't know what it is. I got up in the middle of the night, knelt by my bed, and asked God to speak to me. In that moment, I felt like He was saying, "I called you to ministry." I remembered in ninth grade at our church's summer camp that I had a time with God where I fully committed my life to Him. I wasn't sure if this was a call to ministry then, but God took me back to that moment.

I wrestled with God that night. I did not know what a full-time job in ministry would look like. I had a plan for my life, and now God was changing that plan. After hours of prayer, tears, and frustration, it really came down to a matter of obedience. Would I trust God? Would I submit to His will for my life? The business job held money and (I thought) stability, but businesses and jobs come and go. God was calling me to a life of faith and trust. I didn't know how I would support myself, but I had to trust in the One who would be my Provider. This was a defining moment in my life.

I went into the business the next day and thanked them for flying me there, then told them I felt like God had other plans for my life. They were nice about it, and in a strange way, I had peace. I didn't know what the future held, but I did walk out trusting God. I knew He had a plan, and I was ready to follow Him.

In a short time, a church called and asked if I would consider working with middle school and college students. I thought, "Middle schoolers. That would be crazy." But I went that first night, and I knew this was what God had called me to do. I loved the students and soon found myself being a student pastor serving with hundreds of middle school, high school, and college students. I loved it! It was what I was created to do. I loved teaching, discipling, and seeing students come to know and grow in Jesus. It was so exciting to see God working in the hearts and lives of students, parents, and leaders. I was overflowing with joy each day, and so thankful that God would call and allow me to serve Him.

After I had been a student pastor for ten years, God called my wife, Lisa, and me to plant a church. I had a great job (with a salary and this amazing thing called "benefits"), so I was not as excited about the call as I should have been. I prayed for clarity and talked with many of my mentors and friends. Lisa and I had hours of conversation and prayers about it. Then, it became a matter of obedience and not success. Ultimately, it didn't matter if it worked or not. What mattered was whether we would be obedient to God's call.

I remember quoting Philippians 4:6–7 over and over, "Don't worry about anything, but in everything, through prayer and petition with thanksgiving, let your requests be made known to God. And the peace of God, which surpasses every thought, will guard your hearts and minds in Christ Jesus." I knew that if this was what God called us to do, then He would accomplish His will. If you can do it without an ounce of faith, then it is probably not of God.

If you can do it without an ounce of faith, then it is probably not of God.

On a Thursday night twenty years ago, fifteen people gathered in an apartment clubhouse for a Bible study. What started then became a journey few of us could have ever imagined. Today, the church that God was launching that night, Rolling Hills Community Church, has grown to impact many lives both in Middle Tennessee and around the world. In addition, God has blessed us with an amazing church body whom I truly love.

What started in that apartment clubhouse has grown to be a large, multifaceted ministry. And that ministry requires a substantial infrastructure. We gather in a 143,000-square-foot building, with three tenants. The monthly income from these tenants pays the mortgage on our building. God has also blessed us with three other large buildings in and around the Nashville area. These buildings host our other campuses and a nonprofit mission ministry called Justice & Mercy International, which provides housing and care for orphaned and vulnerable children in Moldova. Our ministry also has a mission center in the middle of the Amazonian jungle for pastor trainings as well as two boats for taking medical, dental, and mission teams to remote villages throughout the jungle. We also have two Learning Centers with more than 350 children in weekday programs.

God has moved in a mighty way, and I am simply in awe of Him. All glory to Him. It has also taken an incredible team of staff and lay leaders, plus a lot of work and business principles, to navigate and to manage. Our God is so faithful, and it continues to be an amazing journey. Every day I wake up and say, "Thank You, Father, and what are You going to do today?" Our God is so good, and every day I grow more excited about what He is doing.

Ministry's Need for Business

When God first called me into ministry, what surprised me most was how much business was involved in the work. My first month at the church was during budget season. I found myself looking at revenue and expenses from the prior year and then needing to make budget projections for the coming year. The calendar planning also needed dollars allotted for each event. I thought, "I'm a pastor. I just want to love and help people, and here I am doing business." Since I had majored in business in college, I did have some knowledge to draw from in the process. So much of ministry is business. In fact, the most effective ministries, I have discovered, are the best-run organizations. If you and your organization are going to succeed, you need to learn and grow in the business side of ministry.

Yet, in seminary, I did not have one business class. I had some wonderful theological training, and I am grateful for my time in seminary, but I wish there had been resources to help prepare me for the real world of ministry. This is why in my first ministry job I was so surprised to find out how much time the business side actually consumes. Creating a ministry budget and understanding how it fits in the overall church or nonprofit budget is essential. My job also included booking mission trips, camps, and retreats with payments from kids and adults. I had to learn about travel insurance and specific budgets for each trip. I had to hire employees and interns. I had to know about contract staff, employment laws, and benefits. Add to this my own personal financial decisions—W-2 employment, self-employment, retirement, disability, and supplemental insurance. I tried to get advice from other pastoral staff, only to find that this was an area in which they struggled.

The business knowledge needed for my first staff position was more than I expected, and yet it paled in comparison to the business knowledge that is required for church planting. When God called Lisa and me to plant a church, I quickly realized that we were not only planting a church, but in the eyes of the law, we were essentially starting a small nonprofit organization. There were incorporation documents to draw up, bylaws to write, tax-exempt status to file, bank accounts to set up, leases to read, web presence to establish, business cards to design and print . . . and so much more. You needed to have some understanding of legal, IT, HR, banking, and accounting—or at least know people who did.

I remember thinking, "All I want to do is to tell people about Jesus and help those in need, but I am spending a lot of time establishing good business principles." I quickly realized how thankful I was that God allowed me to major in business! Throughout my ministry career, the business background helped prepare me just as much for what God was going to do in me and through me. From student ministry to senior pastor and nonprofit leader, ministry board leader, and launching a private Christian preschool, among other roles—the business background God gave me has been invaluable, and I pray I can pass on some of this wisdom that I have gained through the years to help you as well.

What Our World Needs Today

We desperately need a thriving church and ministries in our society. We need spiritual influence today more than ever. It is the teachings of Jesus that call us to take care of the poor and needy. It is the influence and impact of Jesus that show us the importance of building strong marriages and families. It is the influence and impact of Jesus that call us to justice and racial reconciliation in our cities and communities.

Governments can't do it. Businesses can't do it. Both are important, but they can't change the human heart. Only God and His power working through people can do that. The need is so great. Just look at 9/11. Or economic downturns. Or the mental health crisis coming out of COVID. When people needed help and healing spiritually, mentally, and emotionally, the government couldn't respond. The government and businesses don't know what to do, and again, it is the church and Christian ministries that are stepping in to provide counseling, care, help, and hope that people so desperately need today.

Revival Is Coming

Revival is a movement of God that impacts Christ followers, churches, and communities. Revivals are marked by a return to God. Sometimes revivals in churches lead to spiritual awakenings in our nation. And, I believe, this is coming. The odds may seem overwhelming, but remember, this is where God does His greatest work. As followers of Christ, and for every Christ-centered ministry, we need to be ready. We need to prepare now. It's not hard to see that government and businesses can't fix our world or an individual's heart. Everyone needs the Lord. And when people are confronted with their own mortality, where do they turn? When major events happen in our world, where do people look for meaning and purpose in life? The only true answer is Jesus. Money, power, and success will never completely satisfy. It is in these times of crisis, war, and fear that we discover our deep need for God.

As we prepare for this coming revival, we must be wise. We need to learn, build, and grow. There is so much ministries can learn from business. Our God is a God of order and structure, systems and organization. Look at the universe, the world, and even the human body. Businesses have taken these principles and applied them well. The church has so much to learn and to apply in order to have a greater impact for the glory of God. Let's be ready when revival comes.

There are two main challenges ministries and nonprofits are up against today. The first is getting started—or restarted. How can we plant a church, add a new ministry, multiply, or expand organizationally for new growth? We will talk more about that in chapters 7 and 8. The second challenge has to do with buildings and space. We need spaces to gather and to do ministry. But buildings are exorbitantly expensive. Finding a place to meet for church or do a local ministry or even have office space is a struggle for most churches and nonprofits. As cities grow, churches and ministries often can't afford to get into the real estate market. But what if God was providing a way? What if God has already been answering this prayer? There are hundreds of church buildings in every major US city. There are thousands of warehouses, movie theaters, schools, and more that are sitting empty or are being under-utilized all across the country.

This presents an incredible opportunity, but we must know how to utilize these spaces. If ministries can learn business principles and practices, then these transferable principles will help ministries be even more effective in the greater work. Let's learn to grow the ministry He has entrusted to us and implement these principles so we can maximize the impact for God's kingdom!

Chapter 2

BUSINESS PRINCIPLES MATTER

The ability to manage the business side of ministry effectively makes or breaks an organization. The most effective leaders and pastors understand the importance of running a church, ministry, or nonprofit well on the business side. However, business is rarely, if ever, a part of theological education. Even aspiring social workers have very little business training.

We all are stewards of the resources and money God has entrusted to us personally, but pastors and ministry leaders are also stewards of the resources given by their constituents. Everyone in ministry must learn and grow in their financial responsibility in order to handle God's resources effectively. In fact, the better leaders are at handling the business side of their ministry, the greater the impact they can make in the lives of people and for the kingdom of God.

I want you to make a significant difference in your community. I truly believe that churches and nonprofits can change the world by transforming families, communities, cities, and countries with the grace and love of God.

The same power that raised Jesus from the dead is alive in us. The same power that launched the early church and this movement that swept the world is still at work today. The early church learned from Jesus and implemented business practices to organize the church. The Holy Spirit was transforming lives, and the disciples were organizing the ministry. From taking care of widows to evangelism, discipleship, and taking up offerings, the early church was run well, and God was glorified through that work. He is ready to move again today.

Sometimes when we talk about business, it may seem like it shouldn't be associated with the church and nonprofit ministry. After all, Jesus drove the money changers out of the temple in anger (Matt. 21:12–13). But this was because they were abusing the people and hindering them from worship. The money changers were overcharging the people, and this was at the heart of Jesus' anger. Jesus wanted people to come unhindered to His "house of prayer." However, other times Jesus teaches us about how we should "give back to Caesar the things that are Caesar's, and to God the things that are God's" (Mark 12:17). Jesus watched people put their gifts into the offering basket and commended the widow for giving "all she had to live on" (Mark 12:41–44). Jesus teaches us about being good stewards with what we have been given. Ministry and business are not mutually exclusive; in God's order they go together.

Ministry and business are not mutually exclusive; in God's order they go together.

Learning a New Language

Often when we use business terms—margin, revenue, expenses, return on investment—it can sound like we are speaking a different language. But we need to learn some of this language in order to be more effective in our calling. We do not need a master's in business, but we do need to be proficient in the basics. When we go on mission trips and do ministry in another country, we endeavor to learn the language in order to more effectively help the people and share the gospel. Understanding the language of business can help do the same for ministry.

God values His created order, and He desires for His church to be rightly ordered and organized as well. Yet sometimes churches and non-profits do not spend the time needed to build the infrastructure for the system to run well. We can do greater ministry when we are organized and structured for sustained success.

We should study well-run businesses and learn how they operate. Business is simply the practice of bringing together resources in a system to accomplish a successful result. This is a system, and God's church can learn so much in this area of business. In fact, we should be doing the ministry better than any for-profit business because what we do has both present and eternal ramifications.

In the business world, there is a skill in demand called "systems thinking." This is the awareness of how inputs and actions in one place impact other places in the organization. There is a need for people who understand how decisions in one area impact the whole. The same is needed in the church and nonprofit world as well. Poorly run churches and nonprofits do not make as significant an impact as they could and do not bring honor to the One whose name we proclaim. We must become the best we can become for the glory of God.

It doesn't matter how great the music sounds or how good the teaching is if you can't pay the bills or keep up with your 990 for tax reporting. This is true for all churches and nonprofits. And so many great ministry ideas die because of a lack of business knowledge needed to make the idea a reality. Outside of the calling and grace of God's Holy Spirit, having some knowledge of business is essential for a ministry to thrive.

As the pastor of a church and the president of a nonprofit, I see first-hand the importance of good business practices for doing God's work. There is so much ministry to do—to help the orphaned and the under-served, to share the love of Christ, to grow fully mature disciples, and to strengthen marriages and families. For example, what if there is a new paradigm in ministry and business? What if churches and nonprofits could actually have their buildings paid for by others? This would allow all the money that is given to the church or the nonprofit to go for ministry and missions instead of bricks and mortar. That would be a game changer! Good money management can go toward the building and the spiritual transformation that takes place in the space.

I have seen our God do miracles in the business of ministry. Just like the children of Israel when they entered the promised land and God gave them houses they didn't build and vineyards they didn't plant (Deut. 6:11), I have seen God provide buildings we didn't build and money flow from outside sources. I have seen God do miracles at Rolling Hills Community Church and Justice & Mercy International, and I want to invite you on this journey. I believe God will pour out His blessings when we put Him first, do ministry in a way that honors Him, and use godly wisdom to leverage the business of today to do greater work than ever. Let's learn, grow, and use what God has entrusted to us to further His work in the greatest way possible for His glory.

The Purpose of Planting

God's call and the need in our world compelled us twenty years ago to plant a new church in our community. When we started the church we had no money, no staff, no building. The odds against us seemed overwhelming. But we knew our community and our world needed

Jesus, and He was all about transforming lives and bringing good into our world today.

So often we live on the defensive. We think culture has turned away from God. But we must realize that deep down, everyone is searching for answers to the deep questions of life. Ultimately, everyone needs the Lord. And while it may seem overwhelming to be a part of God's church or a local ministry, the God who did miracles in the Bible is the same God doing miracles today. The God who conquered death is the same God who is always at work in our lives. This is the same God who is always at work in His church.

What are you planting today that will yield a harvest for God's kingdom in the years to come? Maybe it is starting another campus, maybe it is launching a new small group, maybe it is expanding into a new ministry area, maybe it is opening a new department. Whatever it is, plant seeds today in order to yield a harvest for tomorrow. Never stop planting and growing. Things that are alive grow. Our ministry areas should be growing, and the best way to do this is to plant new seeds.

The Business of Ministry Is Life Change in Christ

As churches and nonprofits, we are called to help, love, and serve others. We need to use all the tools and resources God has entrusted to us today. I pray this book will help bring a new movement of church growth and ministry expansion for the glory of our great God. Instead of retreating and living on the defensive, I pray God's church will go forward and others will be impacted for Christ and our world will be changed. Jesus is truly the Hope of the world, so let's all work together to bring Jesus into our neighborhoods, our nation, and our world that is in such desperate need of hope, love, and peace today. There is a lot to learn from business, but we must remember that we are not simply a business—our goal is to share the love of Jesus, serve the least, the last, and the lost, and bring glory to our great God.

Obviously, there are differences between a for-profit business and a nonprofit ministry. While the goal of a for-profit business is to make money, to increase the return for their shareholders, there is also the by-product of providing jobs and helping families. There is a current movement in corporate America toward "CSR," or "Corporate Social Responsibility." There are many businesses that are also actively helping and trying to make a social difference in their community. Business in itself isn't a bad thing; in fact, our American capitalistic society is built on businesses providing jobs and services. Businesses provide jobs for millions of people, and many people's investments and retirement savings are tied to the performance of US businesses and worldwide corporations. For-profit companies can be good, and they make a significant difference, but they lack the power to make the social changes and the eternal impact we all need.

We are not in ministry simply to make money (or we would work in corporate America and make a lot more). Our goal as pastors, executive directors, staff, and ministers is to bring glory to God and to make a difference in the lives of others in the name of Jesus.

We already apply good business practices to running our own homes. In our personal budgets, we watch revenue and expenses. We try not to go into debt on depreciating assets. We aim to maintain a balanced home budget. And when we know it's time to buy a home for our family, we involve real estate agents and lawyers to help us. We can take business practices such as these and apply them in the context of ministry as well.

It is not your church or ministry—it all belongs to God. Sometimes people will ask, "How's your church doing?" I understand what they are saying, but I always try to politely say, "It is God's church and not my church. He has simply allowed me to steward this leadership position for this season." There will be someone else after me, and I pray they can do it even better for the glory of God. There is also an incredible team of people who pour their hearts and souls into doing the work of the Lord. I am simply a steward of what He has entrusted to me. We are all stewards. And, as stewards, we ought to do the best job possible for our Master. Why would we not want to grow His church or ministry and give our best?

Part 2

Possessions
Money & Tangible Assets

Look around—what do you have? What has God entrusted to you to do His work? Money, buildings, people. In business, these are called assets. In ministry, we can call these possessions or resources. We all have something. We live in the wealthiest nation that has ever existed in history. Think about that for a minute. We are doing ministry today with more possessions and resources than any church or ministry before us. And we serve a God who holds all the riches in the world in His hands. He invites us to ask Him for whatever we need. The real challenge, and opportunity, for each of us is how we allocate and invest the possessions and resources our God has entrusted to us.

Chapter 3

THE TENSION BETWEEN BUSINESS & FAITH

I will never forget God calling my wife, Lisa, and me to plant a church. It was scary and exciting at the same time. I already had a great job, yet I knew God was calling me to step out and trust Him and plant a church with no money attached to it or promise of success. We had no buildings or possessions, no equipment or curriculum for children's ministry, AV equipment, or many other resources that are so helpful to having a "church." But I couldn't shake the conviction that God was calling us to plant a church. It finally came down to this—would I trust God? Did I really believe that if God was calling me to this, He would provide?

This is the tension we all face—in church, the nonprofit sector, and our personal lives. We live in a culture that is dominated by the almighty dollar, and while we do need money to live, ultimately we must ask ourselves, "Is our faith and trust in God or in money?"

This is what has kept so many Christ followers from answering the call to full-time ministry or starting something new. This is what has kept churches and nonprofits from expanding existing ministries into new areas and opportunities God is calling them to. We cannot grow comfortable or complacent. We must continue to trust God.

The question of trust demonstrates the tension we all feel between faith and money. God wants us to be wise. He wants us to do our due diligence so that we will succeed and do great things for His glory. He wants us to trust Him, but He also gave us a brain to make wise decisions.

Money does matter. Jesus talks about money almost more than any other topic. Money itself is not bad, like some ministries think it is. It is the "love of money" that creates problems (1 Tim. 6:10). We need to learn to manage money well, but ultimately our faith and trust is in God. There will be times when we don't have enough money, but we must remember that we have a God who holds all the riches of the world in His hands.

Learning to be wise with money is a huge part of understanding the business of running a ministry. But we must always remember to keep God first. It is God who calls us, and it is God who will provide for us. God's math is different from business math. Jesus took five loaves and two fish and fed five thousand men—not to mention all the women and children who were there as well (John 6:1–14). We are called to be wise, prudent, and good stewards, but also to be bold, faithful, and believing God for His best. He truly is the God of miracles. Our God is sovereign, and He loves to bless His people and His work.

There will always be tension between faith and business. Every year, we have this debate in our annual budget meeting. On one side, we have the people who say, "We need to step out in faith, initiate some new programs and hire new staff. Let's just trust the Lord to provide." Yet on the other side, we have people who say, "We need to be wise about how much we increase the budget. We need to study past performance, future projections, and the economic climate of how to use the money God has entrusted to us." What is the answer? Do you budget on faith or on business projections? The answer is YES.

Is there anything God is calling you to do that you are saying, "But I don't have the money"? Put God first and watch Him provide.

Creating a Ministry Budget

One area where we can be wise with money is implementing a budget for our ministries. Even when you are first starting, you need to know how much you need for the ministry to be solvent. This includes any rent, computers, phones, software, office space, employees, and more.

Many of Jesus' parables had to do with business practices. In one particular parable, Jesus says,

> "For which of you, wanting to build a tower, doesn't first sit down and calculate the cost to see if he has enough to complete it? Otherwise, after he has laid the foundation and cannot finish it, all the onlookers will begin to make fun of him, saying, 'This man started to build and wasn't able to finish.'" (Luke 14:28–30)

This parable is primarily about the cost of discipleship, but I also think there's another, smaller message here for builders and planning and making budgets! Counting the cost is the responsible thing to do—in the big and the small. Clearly Jesus knew the cultural importance of financial planning and budgeting—He uses it in a parable about discipleship! So many people skip over this. They feel the call to ministry or to start a new initiative, but it is also so important to take the time to count the cost. If this is not something you are good at or comfortable with, then find someone in your church, a friend, or a volunteer to help you. Later, as the church or nonprofit grows, hire a good accountant or ultimately a chief financial officer. That person is worth it.

Still a Journey of Faith

When Jesus called His first disciples He said, "Follow Me . . ." (Matt. 4:19). Jesus didn't say where He was going or how long they would be gone. He didn't give them a "what to bring" list. He just said, "Follow Me."

Being a disciple is a journey of faith; learning to listen, trust, and obey as we follow Jesus. This means that we will not have it all figured out. There will be times when Jesus calls us to go a different way or do ministry to different groups of people. It is not our church or nonprofit, it is His. Therefore, we must accept the fact that sometimes God simply calls us to step out in faith and there is no possible way to count the cost from a purely human or business perspective. We are called to "walk by faith, not by sight" (2 Cor. 5:7). Yes, that still means you keep a budget to the best of your ability, and you grow in wisdom and spiritual discernment, but you take steps of faith and trust that God will provide.

> *We must accept the fact that sometimes God simply calls us to step out in faith and there is no possible way to count the cost from a purely human or business perspective.*

To walk on water, you must first step out of the boat. When a storm came on the Sea of Galilee one night, all but one of the disciples— Peter—stayed in the boat. Miracles occur when we step out of the boat and follow Jesus. Peter put his life on the line, but he was walking toward Jesus. This is why there will always be tension as we endeavor to balance faith and business: Jesus wants us to never be complacent but always be striving to know Him, follow Him, and make Him known.

Growth requires movement. It has been said that "potential is God's gift to us, and what we do with it is our gift to God."[2] You have been entrusted with a ministry. You have an opportunity to bring glory to God and to impact precious lives with the good news of Jesus. We should want to give our best as an outpouring of love and worship to God.

Peter realized it was safer to be with Jesus on the water than in the boat away from Him. The only struggle for Peter (and for all of us) was keeping his eyes on Jesus. The Bible says, "But when he saw the strength of the wind, he was afraid. And beginning to sink he cried out, 'Lord, save me!'" (Matt. 14:30). But we often do the same as Peter and take our eyes off Jesus and put our focus on our struggles, worries, and fears. Peter did this and began to sink.

Jesus didn't reprimand him, but instead immediately reached out to Peter and pulled him up. Jesus didn't let Peter stay under the water to punish him for his doubts and fears. He didn't walk away. He went directly to Peter and pulled him up. We are so scared to step out of our boat, to start something new for the glory of God, that we forget that Jesus is right there with us the entire time. Ultimately, we can't fail! Even when we stumble, Jesus is there to pull us up.

In what area is Jesus calling you to step out of the boat? Is He calling you to a new ministry? Is He calling you to start something unique and different for His glory? Is He calling you to take a step of faith? Keep your eyes on Jesus. He is always with you.

Modern-Day Fish & Loaves

I will never forget when we were a five-year-old church, with an average age in our congregation of twenty-seven. By this time, we were meeting at a movie theater. We met in the theater for five years and never had a contract. God always provided, and we were completely dependent on Him each and every Sunday. We went through four different general managers at the theater, but always had a place. Setup and tear-down of ten theaters every Sunday—babies in one theater, preschoolers in another, kids' ministry in one, and middle school, high school, and college each had their own. Then we had worship in the largest theater. It was an amazing undertaking every Sunday morning. We had baptisms in a horse trough in the lobby while the ushers were popping popcorn, and if my sermon went long, then they would begin running the movie previews! Every week was an adventure.

After several years, we knew we needed to be somewhere else, but land in our area was expensive. In some places it was a million dollars an acre. Hard to find a place to build or rent. But we kept praying and looking. We had realtors and people in the congregation constantly on the lookout for any place we could go.

One day a woman on our finance team said that she had a client at her bank who owned a warehouse. It had been the old Georgia Boot factory. When he bought it, they had cleared everything out, so it was simply a giant empty box. The building was on the market for $7.2 million. It sat on thirteen acres just south of the downtown area. When she told us about it, we laughed. How in the world could we ever afford this? We had only a few thousand dollars in the bank. But we agreed to talk with him.

When we met the seller, we found out that he was a Christian. He said, "I have heard of Rolling Hills, and it sounds like God is doing some big things there. When I bought this warehouse, I thought that God had a plan for us." It was so encouraging to hear him say this. We told him we did not have a lot (really, any) money, but we were interested. He said, "I will give you $700,000 to use for the down payment." Wow—miracle #1. But that still meant the price for the building was $6.5 million.

We walked away thinking this couldn't happen. But as we continued looking, nothing else seemed to fit. Finally, we called everyone to pray and fast and said, "In a month, after praying and fasting, we are going to take a onetime offering on a Sunday. Please pray and stretch, and let's see what God will do."

I will never forget that next Sunday morning in Theater 15 of Carmike Cinemas. We put a metal wheelbarrow down front in the theater. We prayed and came ready, all trusting God with our lives and with His church. As we closed the service, we invited people to come forward, and all our kids came first. We had forty or fifty kids who came up to the wheelbarrow with their piggy banks. Instead of reaching into their piggy banks and pulling out a few coins and dropping them into the wheelbarrow, they began to pour their entire piggy banks into the wheelbarrow. The sound of those coins hitting that metal reverberated throughout the entire theater. It is a sound I will never forget, and it brought us all to tears. Then all the adults came up and gave our best to the Lord.

Our finance team—nine laypeople in the church who have a background in banking, business, HR, and the like—stayed afterward to count the money. They called me that afternoon and said, "You will never believe this, but the church just gave $1 million." I thought they were kidding. "No way," I exclaimed. "Yes," they reassured me. It was the fish and the loaves all over again. You put what you have into the hands of Jesus and watch Him multiply it, and He truly did! Miracle #2.

We went back to the seller and said, "Well, we now have some money. Is your building still for sale?" He said, "Well, I did not think you were still interested, so I went out and secured three leases for the building. The State of Tennessee wants 10,000 square feet—all of the foster care for Williamson County will come through this building. Comcast wants 10,000 square feet for offices and a hundred parking spots for their trucks, and Naxos, the largest distributor of classical music, wants 30,000 square feet. These are all ten-year, no out leases with AAA-credit tenants. I haven't built out the space, but I have the signed leases."

We stood there thinking. That was 50,000 square feet of leases, but it still left over 90,000 square feet that we could use for the church. So we asked him, "Will you sell us the building?" He said yes. Then we asked, "Will you also give us the leases and we will build them out?" Again, he said yes. And then we asked, "Will you still give us the $700,000 you said you would earlier?" And . . . "Yes." Miracle #3.

However, we still needed to go to some banks to borrow the rest of the money for the building and to build out the tenants. Again, a woman on our finance team who worked at a bank helped prepare an amazing presentation. Just like when you want to borrow money to buy a house, we had to find the right banking partner. We went to nine different banks in one day, and eight of them said, "Five-year-old church, average age twenty-seven? I don't think we are interested." But the last bank we went to visit (we stopped and prayed outside before we walked in) had a banker who sat and listened to our entire presentation. He never asked a question, but at the end he said he would get back to us. We left discouraged but with a little glimmer of hope. A few days later, we called him back, and he said, "I have one more signature, and then I will give you a loan commitment." Miracle #4.

By God's incredible grace, we were able to borrow the money and to build out the warehouse as our new church home. We had a guy in the church who was an owner's rep building contractor. He took over and ran the project. We built out the leases first while we stayed in the movie theater for another year. Then, we built out the space for the church. What is so amazing about all of this is that the rent from our three tenants covered the mortgage on the building. We are in the building that God paid for. Now the money the church puts in could go to ministry and missions. Miracle #5.

Today, this warehouse serves as our central campus. Our God is truly a God of miracles. There is nothing He cannot do. So, whatever you are facing, never forget that. He can do "above and beyond all that we ask or think" (Eph. 3:20). We have seen Him do this so often. Be wise, but always step out in faith. God has an incredible journey planned for you as you follow Him.

The key is to hold tight to God. He does big things like the warehouse, but He also does the small everyday miracles of sustaining His ministry and our lives. I can remember in the early days of the church sitting on the one couch we had in our small rented office and opening the mail on New Year's Eve. I was praying there would be a check so we could make payroll for our three staff members at the end of the year (and praise God, there was!). I can remember asking our few staff to wait to cash their checks, so we could have a few days for money to hit the account. Whether in big ways or small ways, our God is always working. Therefore, stay faithful in the good times and the challenging times because there can always be a miracle coming.

Chapter 4

MINISTRY TAKES MONEY

Our first mission trip to Moldova cost over $36,000. Our church budget for that entire first year was $50,000. We could have said, "There is no way! This is too much money, and we don't have it." We could have backed out. But I'm so glad we didn't (and there are so many kids in Moldova whose lives have been impacted who are glad we didn't too). We prayed, planned, and sent out support letters to family and friends across the country, and God provided as only He can.

About three years later, when we realized that once the kids turned fifteen and had to leave the orphanage and had no place to go, we felt God giving us an answer. Again, it came down to money and more faith. We found a house in Chisinau, Moldova—the capital—that was a big house. We knew we could house at least fifteen girls there with house parents, and it was in a safe area of town. The only problem was it was $250,000.

As a church, we were still meeting in a movie theater. We did not even own property for ourselves, and yet God was calling us to buy a house in Moldova. A quarter of a million dollars is a lot of money. We began to pray, plan, and cast the vision for people to be involved. And miraculously, over time, God provided. The owners of the house in Moldova were Christians, and they knew God had a plan for their home. They were excited about our vision to help orphaned and vulnerable children from their own country, and they even helped us out with the purchase of their home.

Today the work in Moldova is incredible. In 2008, we were able to start our own nonprofit called Justice & Mercy International. Through JMI, we purchased the homes in Moldova and expanded the work of ministry in this country we love. Today, JMI has forty-five full-time local staff in Moldova working with children—social workers, psychologists, vocational directors, nurses, house parents, and more. We have over a thousand kids who are being sponsored and cared for in forty-two different villages throughout the entire country. And we now have four Transitional Living Homes—two for girls and two for boys—with money raised to build two more. We have over a hundred Transitional Living and Independent Living students who are thriving in high school and college, learning English, and being discipled in Christ Jesus. God is truly transforming lives for His glory, and we count it a joy and blessing to be a small part. We've helped kids like Elena, Tudor, Igor, Ala, Inga, Olicia, and countless more who are so special to us. Many of them now have children of their own.

Overcome the Fear of Asking for Money

Fulfilling dreams takes money. There are many people who have great dreams that never become a reality because they are not able to secure the funding. Yet many in ministry have a fear of asking people for money in the first place. We must learn to overcome this fear if we are to grow.

So many ministry leaders are afraid to ask for money. People are afraid they will offend their constituency or dilute their mission. Pastors, especially, struggle with this. If you are the leader of a ministry, then you must embrace the fact that one of your primary roles is to raise money. People have it and they will give, but a leader must cast a compelling vision. Leaders of churches and nonprofits must overcome this fear of asking for money in order to do greater ministry. In the following sections, we'll look at some guiding principles for securing funding as well as maintaining funding for ministry.

The Use of Capital Campaigns

A very effective and strategic way to raise money for specific ministry initiatives is the use of capital campaigns. I have led our church and our nonprofit through several capital campaigns. By God's grace, every one of our campaigns has collected even more money than what was originally pledged. When your ministry identifies the next needed initiative through the strategic planning process, presenting your congregation or constituency with a specific goal and time frame can rapidly grow the organization. Capital campaigns can raise a large amount of dollars in a short amount of time. There are proven techniques that can make a capital campaign very effective and help grow your ministry.

What is the big need for your church or nonprofit that God has put on your heart? Begin to talk and share this with others to see if they feel the same way. Then, to discern the Lord's leading, pray about launching a capital campaign in your church or ministry to fulfill this dream. Before you launch, I encourage you to study other churches or ministries. I have learned so much from looking at websites as well as visiting other churches to see what they do. (We take our Lead Team once every other year to visit other churches—it is so insightful and the churches we visit are always so gracious. It helps us to remember we are all on the same team!) In addition, I encourage you to talk to a church consultant in this area. In our personal lives we will find a financial advisor, so in our ministry lives we need to be open to learning more from the professionals who specialize in this arena. There are some great resources available to you. Overall, the key is to identify the specific needs that you feel God is calling you to as a church or nonprofit that are over and above your annual operating budget, and then put together a plan to pray through and raise the needed money. Remember, "Nothing will be impossible with God" (Luke 1:37).

Recently, God gave us a call to have a new boat in the Amazon. Mary Katharine Hunt is our executive director for Justice & Mercy International, and when she was working with our national director in the Amazon, Sarah Rodrigues, they knew we needed a new boat. We had an existing boat, but it was too small and could not make trips too far into the deeper regions of the Amazon. We were now doing ministry in forty of the fifty-six provinces of the Amazon, and we needed a boat that would be big enough to take more teams and do ministry. We needed to have a kitchen, places for hammocks for teams to sleep, rooms for doctors and dentists, places to store food and clothes to give out, and places for teams to gather to eat meals and have devotionals.

This boat would have to be custom built and would cost about $500,000. At first, we thought, "No way." But then we remembered our God. If God was calling us to do this, then He would provide. We set out to build a "capital campaign" around this boat. We prayed and cast the vision. God moved, and people responded—and in just about six months, all the money was raised and construction began on the boat.

By God's grace, I had the chance to take my entire family on the inaugural trip of our new boat. We had seventy people with us—forty from our church at Rolling Hills in the States and thirty other Christ followers with Justice & Mercy Amazon in Brazil. We had doctors, nurses, children's leaders, pastors, cooks, boat crew, translators, and more. We left from Manaus and headed up the Amazon River. We slept in hammocks under mosquito netting and would wake up in a different village each morning. It was incredible. The villagers lined up to see the doctors and nurses. We gave out clothes and food, shared Bible stories, and played games with the children. We were tired and exhausted and yet overwhelmed with the love of the people and the beauty of the jungle. At night, we ate dinner and then all gathered for devotional times on the top deck of the boat to look at the stars and worship.

The boat, the *Splendor*, is incredible. We do mission trips all throughout the Amazon. We have Study & Serve trips for women and Fishing & Serve trips for men. Our ministry to the villages has expanded exponentially. Lives are being impacted because of people's generosity and God's call on our lives.

People want to be a part of something bigger than themselves. When you cast a God-given vision, people will respond. God stirs in the hearts of His people and cultivates generosity. Capital campaigns are so important and effective in helping us further God's mission through ministry. People want to give to something specific that will make a difference, and that is what a capital campaign can help us do. Make it specific. Show people the difference God can make. Be bold and share His story. Then, watch what God will do.

Donor Development

Most churches and nonprofits lag in the area of donor development. Growing donor development for a ministry is essential for the long-term growth and health of the organization. This can be done with volunteers, paid staff positions, and even outside consultants. From recurring donations to estate planning, this has short- and long-term implications. Often, donor development is overlooked in ministry, but developing an ongoing donor program can be learned, and its impact is significant.

In ministry, I believe we struggle with identifying our bigger donors because of what the Bible teaches in the book of James about not favoring rich people over the poor. When it comes to salvation and service, we should never show favoritism—in fact, God does not show favoritism (remember Peter and Cornelius in Acts 10). However, God does give some people the gift of "giving." Just as we help people develop their spiritual gift of teaching, administration, leadership, and more, we should also help people with the gift of giving. Christ followers are called to give. Therefore, identify who in your church or nonprofit are your key givers and then disciple them in this area. Show them the needs and be willing to give them a specific ask. Givers want to know how much money you need. Tell them and then let the Holy Spirit work on their hearts. We love and minister to them whether they give or not, but be willing to identify, present the need, and ask specifically. You will be surprised how people respond. Followers of Christ love to give!

Measuring "ROI"—Return on Investment

You can't do it all. Let that sink in. Every church and nonprofit has a limited amount of time and money. We have an infinite God, but we have limited resources. Therefore, you must decide where you are going to invest the time and money you have been given for maximum impact. There is an "opportunity cost" for everything we do. What you are currently doing might limit the opportunity for you to do something else that may be more effective for the gospel.

Every organization needs to constantly evaluate their ROI. This is difficult for churches and nonprofits. If something is not working, we often don't want to cancel it because it may hurt people's feelings. There are programs or ministries your church or nonprofit may have done for years, but if you're honest, no one new is coming and few are being reached for Christ. The program or ministry is dead, and everyone but a few know it. You must be bold enough to make the hard decision. It is draining financial capital as well as human capital (time, volunteers, energy, etc.). As a leader, you must be willing to make the hard decision to measure the return on investment and do something different.

Recently, we met with a church in our community, and the question was asked by a very kind, faithful older person in the church, "Are we going to keep the toy drive?" "Are we going to keep Wednesday night suppers?" "What about handbells?" I listened to the questions and thought, "Well, all of these were effective at this church at one point in time, but the church is dying. This is like rearranging chairs on the *Titanic*." It was clear there was sweet emotional concern for these programs, but they were obviously not working. They were not reaching anyone for Christ or growing fully mature disciples. They were taking time and money that could be allocated somewhere else for a greater impact. It's hard to say no or to move on from failing programs, but we must if we are going to truly make a difference.

There is a "sunk-cost bias" that makes these decisions even more challenging. We have a tendency to double down on poor decisions because we don't want to admit that we've made a mistake, or we feel we cannot let the money or time we have already spent be "wasted," or we don't want to hurt someone's feelings. But the truth is you must make the best decision possible for the given moment. This takes humility and faith. As Christians, we know God is ultimately in control, and He can take what we learned from a past investment or ministry and use it for future growth. The world doesn't have this freedom that faith provides, so let's let go of "sunk costs," trust God, and honestly measure the rate of return on everything we're currently doing. But, when we do this, we must be sensitive to the people who have invested so much time and money into a certain program. As leaders, we owe it to them to share why we are making the change and encourage them to be a part of the new ministry because it will have a greater impact on lives for Christ Jesus.

We must ask the hard questions. How much time and money do the current programs we have take, and are they reaching anyone for Christ? So many church buildings have a baptistry that is never used. Why? Because we are allocating time and money in ineffective ways. What percentage of a donation is actually going to help a child or someone in need? Without evaluation, dollars are wasted and ministry is ineffective.

Every business is constantly looking at their ROI, and as churches and nonprofits, we can learn from them in order to have greater ministry impact.

Financial Accountability

As you look at churches and nonprofits throughout history, what will often bring a ministry down is problems over money. Study many great large churches or nonprofits and see how many have completely gone away because they mishandled money. You can be doing a lot of things right, but if you do this wrong (or it is perceived that you are mishandling money as a ministry), then all the years of hard work will be over in an instant. It doesn't matter what position you have in your organization, handling money with integrity and transparency is essential to your job and to the long-term success of the ministry.

> *It doesn't matter what position you have in your organization, handling money with integrity and transparency is essential to your job and to the long-term success of the ministry.*

When we first started as a church, I knew this was an area where we needed the utmost oversight and accountability. Our first team was a finance and administration team. We prayed for and handpicked seven people to be on this team. They all had some financial background and helped us in the budgeting process and overseeing the incoming revenue and outgoing expenses. I wanted to be aware of what was happening but not be the one responsible for touching the cash or the only one having access to the money.

Ministries and churches have a fiduciary responsibility as well as a higher calling to financial transparency. There must be an extreme degree of accountability. Two of the most common reasons people are let go from their jobs at nonprofits and churches are financial and sexual misconduct. People who give to a ministry or to a church are giving out of obedience to God. Therefore, we must be good stewards of the money that a single mom puts in an offering basket the same as that of the rich businessman. Surrounding yourself with people who can hold an organization financially accountable is wise. Relying on a board of directors, elders, or whatever group you have in leadership is best practice.

In addition, there is a time when it is good to have someone outside of the organization review the books. We have an audit of the church and our nonprofit every year. This means we bring in an outside tax firm to go over our financial accounts. Many churches or nonprofits may not be able to afford this, but even having someone else in the congregation or community who works in accounting or banking look over your books will help provide a level of confidence for your supporters. Find someone, or a team of people, who can help in this area. Now, both Rolling Hills and Justice & Mercy International are a part of ECFA, the Evangelical Council for Financial Accountability. This organization requires an outside audit, but this gives our donors a lot of confidence that their gifts to the Lord are being handled with character and integrity.

Financial accountability is to keep you above reproach. Most every Christ follower would never willingly misuse a church's or nonprofit's money. The point of financial accountability is to eliminate any possibility of this happening and to protect what God has entrusted to us. When we first started the church, I knew I did not want to handle the money. I wanted to know what was being given and how much we had to work with in ministry, but I wanted someone else over the money. Since we could not afford any staff at the time, I asked a small team of volunteers who were in business to oversee the money. This was a wise decision, and today, even with staff over finances, we still have a team of laypeople in the church who provide accountability.

Here are other practical steps you can take in this area:

- Always have two signers on checks.
- As a ministry leader, do not use a personal credit card for ministry expenses—keep these separate.
- Be very careful about handling ministry cash. I understand there are times like Sunday morning offerings or international mission trips or petty cash situations where this may be necessary, but do your best to never be the only one responsible for cash from the organization.
- Use a financial program on your phone to take a picture and log all your receipts.

In short, always handle money with integrity and be above board. There are no gray areas on this.

Debt

Is it okay for a church or a nonprofit to have debt? Overall, debt is not good. As the Bible says, "The borrower is a slave to the lender" (Prov. 22:7). For the most part, we should do the best we can to avoid debt individually and as a ministry.

Debt is essentially trading future money for money now. Without debt, most people could never afford to buy a house. Then, as they pay it off, it essentially becomes a savings account. Debt is something that must be managed and only entered into on an appreciating asset and after much prayer and wise counsel. While you should never go into debt on a depreciating asset, there are times when debt can help springboard an organization to a new level. If you go into debt to buy a new church building or a new ministry center, then there should be a plan to pay back this money as quickly as possible. "Debt tolerance" is something every church and nonprofit needs to address. For example, I talked with a large church who had the opportunity to buy land to build a new church building. They prayed about it and worked with a bank to secure a very low interest rate. They went to the church and raised the down payment. They bought the land, built the building, and have grown exponentially in reaching many in their community for Christ. They built into their budget a debt repayment plan, and after twenty years are now debt free. Sometimes God gives us opportunities, but we must be wise when it comes to debt. We serve Him first, so we must learn to be content with what He has entrusted to us. Debt can be dangerous, so using debt wisely is important in all areas of your life and ministry.

Annual Reports

Corporations send an annual report to their shareholders. This is a great practice for churches and nonprofits as well. An annual report or another method of sharing the financial numbers with your constituency is an important way to increase giving because people can see how their donations are being used. Annual reports are a great way to celebrate all the ministry that has happened throughout the year as well as to cast the vision for the upcoming year.

Many people find numbers boring or confusing. Part of being transparent is in how you present information. It should be clearly communicated. In your reports, include visuals like charts and graphs as needed. This helps keep people excited and informed about where their money is going.

Every year at Rolling Hills and Justice & Mercy International, we send out an annual report to those who have invested in the ministry.

This is always so exciting, as we have a chance to highlight what God has done in the ministry throughout the year. This also shows people where their money is going and how it is being used in ministry to accomplish God's work. We use this annual report to communicate vision and to continue to invite people to join in God's work.

This is also a great time and a great way to say thank you to those who invest in God's work at your church or nonprofit. It is a great opportunity to thank your "donors" and to let them know how much they are valued. People need to feel appreciated. Many churches and nonprofits never thank their people. If people are never thanked, then after a while they stop giving because they don't feel needed. How can you value and honor the "giving" leaders in your organization? People are committed to your organization, and this is why they give, but saying thank you affirms their investment and makes them feel good about giving in the future.

It Doesn't Take Much

Our church recently met with a bank to present a proposal for a new expansion project. We had taken the time to think through what the bank might need for budget numbers, giving units, assets, and liabilities. The bank representative responded, "Most proposals we see from churches are usually on the back of a napkin." Churches and nonprofits must do better than this. An easy way is to work with an outside CPA firm or a similar consultant. Usually, there is someone in this line of work who is already involved in the church.

In Matthew 25, Jesus tells us that we will all stand before God one day and must give an account of our lives. Jesus talks about the separation of the sheep from the goats, then goes on to say,

> "Then the King will say to those on His right, 'Come, you who are blessed by My Father, inherit the kingdom prepared for you from the foundation of the world. For I was hungry and you gave

Me something to eat; I was thirsty and you gave Me something to drink; I was a stranger and you took Me in; I was naked and you clothed Me; I was sick and you took care of Me; I was in prison and you visited Me.' Then the righteous will answer Him, 'Lord, when did we see You hungry and feed You, or thirsty and give You something to drink? When did we see You a stranger and take You in, or without clothes and clothe You? When did we see You sick, or in prison, and visit You?' And the King will answer them, 'I assure you: Whatever you did for one of the least of these brothers of Mine, you did for Me.'" (Matt. 25:34–40)

From what Jesus says, it doesn't take much. A cup of water, some food, clothes, visiting the sick or those in prison. Yes, ministry takes money, but it really is about offering the little, or much, that we have and investing it in the things that truly matter. Money is a tool to help us accomplish the work of God: caring for those in need and loving and serving others. When we do this, then we further bring heaven to earth as Jesus taught us to pray, "Your kingdom come. Your will be done on earth as it is in heaven" (Matt. 6:10). This is our call. We don't concentrate on how much money we do or don't have; we concentrate on doing what God has called us to do, stewarding well what He has given us, and He will supply what we need. Will we invest what He gives us to have maximum impact for His glory?

Part 3

People

Empowering People & Reaching Communities

In any ministry, it's not the leader's job to do it all. So many times, we think it is. In the early days of planting the church, I worked endless hours. There were times I was exhausted. Then, I had to come to a point to realize that what I was doing was not healthy for me, for my family, or even for the church.

You may remember from the story of Moses about there being a point in his life when he was about to burn out. God used him to lead a million-plus people out of Egypt. He saw God do miracles! Yet, he was trying to do it all himself. When his father-in-law, Jethro, came to visit, and Moses told him that he decided all the disputes between his people and taught them God's laws, Jethro said, "What you're doing is not good" (Ex. 18:16–17). Jethro then gave Moses a lesson on delegation that ended up sustaining Moses and the people of Israel.

If we are trying to do everything ourselves, then what we're doing is not good. We must learn to delegate and empower others to do the work of ministry. If we do it all ourselves, we are depriving people of the opportunity to grow in their own personal journey with the Lord. We are limiting the growth of the ministry area we lead. As spiritual leaders, we are called to engage and empower our people.

Chapter 5

INVOLVING OTHERS IN GOD'S WORK

I'm writing this section on a plane coming home from the Holy Land. Every two years, I lead a group from our church to Israel on a Biblical Study Tour. It is amazing! What a privilege to make this pilgrimage to the Land. I love hiking in the wilderness where the children of Israel walked as God delivered them from being slaves in Egypt. I love going to the Dead Sea, seeing Masada, and reading the Psalms in En Gedi. I love spending time at the Sea of Galilee and studying the Gospels where Jesus called His first disciples. But what is always impressive and jaw-dropping to me is being in Jerusalem. Going to the Temple Mount, the Via Dolorosa, and the Garden Tomb renews and inspires my faith in Jesus, our Messiah, every time.

The Temple Mount was where Solomon built the first building in the center of the city for the glory of God. David and Solomon longed to build a place for people from all over to come and worship. David was living in a palace in Jerusalem and said to the prophet Nathan, "Look, I am living in a cedar house while the ark of God sits inside tent curtains" (2 Sam. 7:2). God's presence was residing in the tabernacle at the time.

God put on David's heart this desire and vision not just to build his own palace, but to build a temple for his God. This is an awesome vision! So often we want to build our own kingdoms, but are we building God's kingdom?

God told David that he was not the one to build it because he had shed too much blood, but his son Solomon would build it. David began to make preparations to help his son succeed in this assignment. David wanted to build the temple in the highest point of the community, so he went for the holy land where Abraham was going to sacrifice Isaac to the Lord (Gen. 22). The land was then owned by Araunah the Jebusite, who told David that he would give him the land. David responded, "No, I insist on buying it from you for a price, for I will not offer to the LORD my God burnt offerings that cost me nothing" (2 Sam. 24:24). I love David's commitment and passion. He recognized all God had done in his own life, so he wanted to do something great for God that would outlive him—a place for others to worship God for generations.

David was far from perfect; in fact, he had some huge failings in his life. Yet after all the failures, David repented and God extended to him mercy. David was forgiven much, so he wanted to do something great for God. At the end of David's life, he was called "a man after [God's] own heart" (Acts 13:22 NIV). My prayer is that we would be this dedicated and passionate in our own day.

David had the dream and the vision, but it was his son Solomon who actually built the temple. Solomon organized the building project and invested personally. Solomon was also wise enough to involve some incredibly gifted and skilled people to do the construction. The entire community came together to accomplish the assignment. People gave generously and were involved in the work. Everyone had a part to play, and they invested their hearts and lives as an act of worship.

When the building of the First Temple was completed, the people had an incredible Grand Opening Celebration, complete with the biggest BBQ cookout in the history of the world. And the awesome part was that God moved in. His Spirit was so thick over the temple that the people could not even go in. I think this is a pretty clear affirmation of God's blessing and approval. God showed up! Wouldn't you have loved to have been there?

Solomon's Temple

The temple Solomon built stood from 950 to 586 BC—over four hundred years of people coming and worshiping God in that place. Imagine how many people this impacted, even generations later. In fact, every Jew, regardless of where they lived, was supposed to come to worship at the temple three times a year—on the major feasts. But there were people there every day. The sacrificial system was in place, and Israel prospered in those days as they kept the Lord first, showing generations what was important and essential.

But the people began to drift from God. This is always the problem. They stopped reading the Law and worshiping God alone. So, God told the people through the prophet Jeremiah that as a result, God was going to put them in exile for seventy years. The temple was destroyed in 586 BC by the Babylonians, and the people were carried off into exile. Once you were conquered back then, you were done. Your entire nation was wiped out or absorbed into the stronger nation. But our God always keeps His promises—that's important for us to remember.

The Persians conquered the Babylonians, and Cyrus the Great became the ruler over the empire. Cyrus then issued a decree in 539 BC that the Jews could return to their land (2 Chron. 36:22–23). The Jews returned and began to rebuild their own houses. Haggai the prophet told the people to get their priorities straight (Hag. 1 and 2). Haggai reminded them that they were living in comfortable homes while the house of the Lord, the temple, was in ruins. Yet they were saying, "The time has not come for the house of the LORD to be rebuilt" (Hag. 1:2). The people had decided they were going to rebuild the temple, but after they had everything else in their life perfect (dangerous thinking for all of us as well). The people had good intentions but misguided priorities. Haggai reminded them that their primary concern should be to rebuild God's house.

The people finally listened to the prophet of the Lord and rebuilt God's house. In 516 BC, the temple was completed—seventy years after the First Temple was destroyed (just like God said). Solomon's Temple is known as the First Temple, and the rebuilt temple became known as the Second Temple. Some of the people were upset that the new temple was not as splendid as the old one had been. The Lord spoke to them through the prophet Haggai: "Who is left among you who saw this house in its former glory? How does it look to you now? Doesn't it seem like nothing to you? Even so, be strong. . . . For I am with you. . . . And My Spirit is present among you. . . . The final glory of this house will be greater than the first. . . . I will provide peace in this place" (Hag. 2:3–5, 9).

This temple was the one that Herod the Great added onto, and it became even more grand than the First Temple. This temple stood from 516 BC to AD 70. It was the temple where Jesus was dedicated and where He taught. Jesus prayed and worshiped at the temple. He didn't say there is no need for this, but actually affirmed this by His presence. And it was the temple where Jesus showed that He is our Ultimate Sacrifice, so we don't have to come to worship to bring a lamb, goat, ram, or pigeon to be sacrificed to atone for our sins. Jesus paid the ultimate price. Now, we can come to "His house," and truly make it a time of worship, prayer, and celebration. We are so blessed! And it is obvious that God loves His house.

The Early Church

The early church met in the temple courts. How cool is this? The early church was not a small house church. Yes, "they broke bread from house to house," but they also met in the temple courts (Acts 2:46). They had corporate worship all together, and then they had small groups in homes. Remember after Pentecost, the early church was over three thousand people. It was a megachurch back then. Then, it grew to five thousand men, not including women and children, so many estimate over twenty thousand people. This is a big church. Not just a house church, but both corporate worship (temple courts) and small groups (homes). House churches work for a season, and they especially work throughout the world. We need more house churches, but as the church grows, we need something more for children, students, and specialized ministries. We need places for discipleship, worship, ministries to those in need, weddings, funerals, and community gathering spaces. We need a building.

The Jews already had synagogues that served as church buildings for them. The synagogue would be a house of prayer but also a school for the children. It was the place in the community for worship, prayer, weddings, funerals, school—the building was truly the community center in that particular town. On his mission trips, Paul would always go first to the synagogue of whatever town he was in. Paul taught in the synagogues—this is where he would go to spread Christianity. Buildings have always been important to God and His people.

As Christianity spread throughout the world, Christ followers who have gone before us began to build buildings as places of worship to the one true God. From smaller buildings to larger ones, our world is filled with places of worship built by Christ followers. In fact, some of the most famous buildings in the world are cathedrals and churches built to God. Did you know it took over 182 years to build Notre Dame with over a thousand carpenters, masons, and metalsmiths, and it was completed in 1345? Today, it is still the most visited site in all of France. Michelangelo's greatest work was the designing of St. Peter's Basilica, and it took over 150 years to build. Westminster Abbey was started in 1050 and became an abbey in the late 1100s. The National Cathedral in Washington, DC, was started by President Theodore Roosevelt and took eighty-three years to complete.

All of these buildings are amazing and show so many Christ followers' passion to do something great for God that would impact countless people for Christ and outlive them. But it is not just these incredible buildings, it is the churches that were built in cities and towns all over the world. Built by hand. Built by blood, sweat, and tears because people wanted to bring glory to God in their community. Christians who stood shoulder to shoulder to hoist up lumber, stack bricks, lay mortar, and pray that their children would grow up in this place and do something great for God in their day as well. They prayed, they gave money, they sacrificed, so that God's name would be lifted high in generations to come. Maybe your great-great-great-great-grandparents, your grandparents, or even your parents. And now the generations come to us.

Now It's Our Turn

This is our time today. Not to simply build our own houses and our own little kingdoms, but to build God's house and His kingdom. It is our time to ask God for a vision that will outlast us. To build something great for the glory of God that will impact the next generations! This is our time and opportunity. God's presence is still moving. God's presence is still filling church buildings all over the world today. As Psalm 22:3 says, the Lord is "enthroned on the praises" of His people.

> *It is our time to ask God for a vision that will outlast us.*

Our buildings will all look different. They don't have to be giant cathedrals, but they need to be appropriate to our communities, and they can be buildings that are refurbished. In previous generations, there were not a lot of buildings around. There are a lot of buildings that can be repurposed for the glory of God. Even to the point where—do you remember?—God told the children of Israel, "The LORD your God [will bring] you into the land He swore to your fathers Abraham, Isaac, and Jacob that He would give you—a land with large and beautiful cities that you did not build, houses full of every good thing that you did not fill them with, wells dug that you did not dig, and vineyards and olive groves that you did not plant" (Deut. 6:10–11). Let's pray, give our best, and watch what God will do.

There will always be a need for buildings for churches and ministries. Some people think that the need for buildings is going away and churches will be in homes only. But I disagree. There is power when the body of Christ is gathered. "Where two or three are gathered together in My name, I am there among them" (Matt. 18:20). Meeting in homes for small groups is important. Meeting in homes to start churches is important. But ultimately, as the church grows, there needs to be more community space—space for weddings, funerals, preschools, student and adult Bible studies, and more. Church buildings come in all shapes and sizes. There is no one size fits all. And all are important.

When we were first meeting in a hotel ballroom, someone asked one day, "So, when are we going to have a church?" I responded, "We have a church, do you mean a building?" Renting facilities is a great way to save dollars on infrastructure. When you purchase or build a building, there are so many other costs associated with it. More churches and nonprofits are using rented facilities as a way to reduce overhead and allow more dollars to go to direct ministry. On the other hand, there comes a time when it makes more sense to own instead of rent. When building a facility or buying an existing structure, it is important to consider how to maximize this asset. Can part of the facility be rented? Can additional ministries or community events be hosted in the facility?

As a church, when we moved into this giant warehouse in late 2009, we realized that we had a lot of space—over 90,000 square feet. I prayed that we would be able to use this space more than just on Sunday mornings. So many churches have big buildings, but they are only used for one to two hours a week on a Sunday morning. The building should never be the vision; the vision is the vision. Therefore, when God miraculously provided this big building for us, we made a motto of "Fill it up and wear it out." We were determined to use the building as a tool to reach people for Christ and to grow up fully mature disciples in Christ Jesus. And we knew this was more than just one to two hours on a Sunday morning.

How did we do this? We stayed with two worship services to start. Even though we were in a bigger building, we had this "Worship One, Serve One" mentality—worship one hour on Sunday morning and serve the other hour. This was important because we needed help with preschool, children, students, parking, greeters, ushers, and more. But also, it allowed us to develop people. Jesus said, "The Son of Man did not come to be served, but to serve" (Mark 10:45). Learning to serve is an important part of discipleship.

Next, we began giving away and renting out our building for community events. We host the Breakfast with the Mayors once a quarter with the mayors of our city and county coming together with over three hundred business and community leaders. This is an incredible chance for us to serve alongside our community as well as to introduce new people to God's church here at Rolling Hills. In addition to the mayors' breakfasts, we also host the police graduation for the city. This is such a special time every year. Then we have the Williamson County dance recitals, school graduations, weddings, business conferences, and much more. All of these are such a blessing to have the building be used to reach and impact people, and many of these events provide extra income for our church. These outside rentals are a big part of our strategic vision to impact our community for Christ.

One of the best things we have done as a church is to start the Rolling Hills Learning Center. In addition to using our worship center throughout the week (and not just on Sunday mornings), we also want to use our children's area. There is a great need in our community for early childhood programs. We have many families where both parents work, and they need help with their children during the day.

The Rolling Hills Learning Center started twelve years ago with one classroom for half a day on one day of the week. That's it. Just start. It doesn't have to be big at first—it will grow. But we did start, and boy, are we glad we did. Today, the Rolling Hills Learning Center is a four-days-a-week program with over 250 precious children at our Franklin campus and over eighty children at our Nolensville campus. That is 330 children who are growing up with a spiritual foundation and families who are involved in God's church at Rolling Hills or are being introduced to what it means to have a church "home." We have so many children in the building. They bring joy and laughter, and they keep our church young. In addition, the Rolling Hills Learning Center makes money as additional outside income for the church to take care of the facility, hire amazing teachers, and further greater ministry. We truly feel like we are raising up the next generation in Christ. It is such a blessing, and it's a great way to use the facility to invest in people.

Chapter 6

IT'S ALL ABOUT JESUS & PEOPLE

Ministry is about helping people. Jesus said, "Love the Lord your God with all your heart, with all your soul, and with all your mind. This is the greatest and most important command. The second is like it: Love your neighbor as yourself. All the Law and the Prophets depend on these two commands" (Matt. 22:37–40). Many churches and organizations can drift from this calling and make it about themselves, maintaining their building, or preserving the past.

I had a pastor tell me once that he believed his role was to "preserve the traditional music of the church." Is that really what God wants? Is the traditional music of the church with or without instruments? Gregorian chants? Bells? Hymns or worship music from the '90s? We know God is giving us a "new song" (Ps. 96:1). There will always be new styles of worship music, both in the States and in other countries. Our role is not to preserve a certain style of music, but to grow spiritually mature worshipers of Jesus. Music, buildings, and books are only tools we use to lead others to the throne of God. Our God is alive and active and drawing people to Himself. We must always be focused on loving God and loving others.

As the ministry grows, you need to add volunteers and staff. Effective volunteers are essential to any ministry and church. Recruiting, training, and mobilizing volunteers are the responsibilities of any good leader. However, at some point, you must begin adding paid staff. The question always becomes, "Do you staff into the growth or do you wait for the growth to support a person and then add staff?" The fact is, people reach people. As an organization, you must constantly be moving toward finding and keeping the right people. Once you begin having volunteers and staff, the organization then needs to keep moving people into their areas of strength. A mix of full-time and part-time paid staff along with trained volunteers is how ministries succeed. None of us can do everything. Again, it is important to program to your strengths and staff to your weaknesses. Leaders must constantly bring people around them to help increase the organization's results. When you are in a start-up ministry, you need to access all the people around you. For example, even though I have a business background, I have no clue on the tax side. When we started the church, I asked a friend who is a CPA if he would help. He was amazing! He did so much of the heavy lifting on the tax side to make sure we were compliant. I am so thankful for him! In this chapter, we will create a plan for volunteer and staff development in order for the ministry to be most effective.

The greatest asset of any church or nonprofit, outside of the Spirit of God, is the volunteer. The most effective churches and nonprofits have figured out how best to mobilize volunteers. Ultimately, it takes a great staff team for any church or nonprofit to be successful, but the real value comes in training, equipping, and empowering passionate volunteers.

Investing in Missions and Ministry

Many times, the question we struggle with is, "Do we send money, or do we personally become involved?" We all know we should be helping people in our community, but every organization must examine this question. Are there areas where it is better to support other churches or nonprofits, or do we need to become involved ourselves? We can't do everything, and we have a limited amount of dollars. Evaluating our personal or financial involvement is important. For example, sometimes people question taking large teams on mission trips. "Wouldn't it be better to send the money that the people pay to the country itself?" But as a good friend of mine in Moldova said, "Please come to Moldova. It is not your money we need as much as it is you." When people go, see, and get involved, that is where life change happens; not just for those people being served, but for those who go to serve. The people who go come back and are advocates for the ministry. They are the ones who see the need and then have others join them. This is how growth happens for everyone involved.

Protecting Our People

Just this past week, we had a school shooting in our community. This is something we never thought would happen here, especially at a small private Christian school. We hear about school shootings, but most of us think that we live in a "bubble." But it is very real. And as pastors and nonprofit leaders, we must protect our people physically and spiritually.

The school shooting that took place here was heartbreaking. Three precious children and three godly teachers lost their lives. I can't even imagine the hurt and pain of these families. We have spent these past days counseling and ministering in our church to families and teachers from the school. The long-term implications are enormous for all the children, faculty, and our entire community.

Through it all, there are many ways that people have seen God's presence and the school's preparedness. The school leadership was wise enough to have their teachers and students participate in active shooter drills. For the past two years, the school has had regular security training. They had also simulated gunfire, so the teachers and students would be able to respond in a real event. This training and preparation saved countless lives. The shooter, armed with two AR-15s and a handgun, unloaded close to two hundred rounds in the school for over fourteen minutes. Once the teachers heard the first shots, they went into lockdown in their classrooms. The police were contacted, and they responded. As horrific as the entire situation was, the administration did their part, and they saved children.

We must think about security and how it impacts all of our churches, nonprofits, and gatherings. Yes, it means allocating more money, but it is a must. From armed security guards on-site to training preparations, we must protect our people both physically and spiritually. This includes cybersecurity as well—protecting cash and credit cards is looking after the money God has entrusted to us as well.

Businesses and corporations allocate massive resources to security in their offices as well as cybersecurity. There are many companies out there who will do safety training for schools, churches, and nonprofit organizations. This is worth your time and is essential for the world we live in today. Even with all the security, there will still be ways that criminals can gain access to our databases and people. This is where we pray and prepare. We are in a spiritual battle—this epic struggle between good versus evil. Praying for God's protection and His wisdom is essential.

Nehemiah

The temple was rebuilt and completed in 516 BC, just as God had told His people that they would be in exile for seventy years for their disobedience. But then the walls around the city were not rebuilt for another seventy years. Why? The walls were the dignity and protection of the city. Jerusalem was still in ruins, and the walls needed to be rebuilt. It only took Nehemiah fifty-two days to rebuild the walls (Neh. 6:15). No one had done anything before that.

God is looking for leaders who are willing to step out and do something for His glory. Nehemiah answered that call—will we? It is easier to sit on the sidelines, but God is inviting us to be in the game. This is where the miracles happen. When we hear God's call and step out in faith, we see God do what only He can do. It is not easy, but it is amazing!

The challenges Nehemiah faced doing God's work back then are the same challenges we face today.

1. Accepting God's Call

Nehemiah had a great job. He was successful. He could have enjoyed a comfortable life and just lived and died in the citadel of Susa. But God had a call on his life. We should never grow comfortable or complacent. We must always be ready when God calls us. God is not looking for our ability, but our availability. Nehemiah was not a construction contractor—he was a cupbearer. He did not have any experience, but his heart was broken over what breaks the heart of God and he decided to do something. God works through His people when we are simply obedient to Him. Jesus said, "The harvest is abundant, but the workers are few. Therefore, pray to the Lord of the harvest to send out workers into His harvest" (Matt. 9:37–38).

> **God is not looking for our ability,**
> **but our availability.**

2. Working with the Government

Nehemiah had to work with the king. This was even bolder than we have to be today. If Nehemiah had said or done something wrong, he could have been killed. We must work with city and state officials today. Now, we will not be killed—praise God!—but we may not receive a building permit if we don't do it right. (We must always remember that many of our brothers and sisters in Christ around the world still do put their lives on the line for the gospel. Their boldness and courage should encourage us in whatever we do for the Lord.) Working with building and codes departments, and learning how to do this the right way, is important. Nehemiah was wise in how he dealt with government officials, and so should we be today.

3. Preparing for Adversity

Many people opposed Nehemiah (Neh. 6:1–2). Today, we have people who come against us when we are doing the Lord's work. Maybe it is an individual who is hostile to the gospel or maybe a housing association who doesn't want a church or a nonprofit in their neighborhood.

For example, we have an amazing nonprofit ministry in our community that found a piece of land for a new ministry building. The plans looked great, and we were all excited to see the difference this nonprofit would make serving and helping even more people. However, when the neighborhood adjoining the property found out about their plans, they petitioned them to stop. They didn't want people who needed help coming to their area. It was sad, but the nonprofit handled it with such grace. They listened, but they didn't stop working. They continued to see God provide, and they continued with their plans. After two long years of working with government officials and the housing community, they were able to break ground recently. It is so exciting to see, and the neighborhood is now supportive of their work. As Nehemiah said, "I am doing a great work and cannot come down" (Neh. 6:3). Understand that there will be adversity, but don't let it stop you from doing the work God has called you to do.

4. Involving People

Ministry is never just about you. Nehemiah could not do this alone. He had to cast the vision and get the people on board. And he did a great job at this! Even having someone rebuild the "dung gate" (Neh. 2:13)—now, that is a smelly job! Don't say no for people. People want to be involved with what God is doing. And don't try to do it all yourself. You can't! Nor should you. The wall was estimated to be 2.5 miles long, so this was truly a God-sized assignment that needed everybody. In any project, a good project manager knows you can build support and buy-in from people by assigning them tasks on a project. If they have played a part, their hearts are more likely to be in the work they are supporting. They will know that they are needed for the project, and they will yearn for its success.

5. Giving Glory to God

The book of Nehemiah has more prayers recorded in it than any other book in the Bible. There is a dependency on the Lord. Nehemiah writes, "We prayed to our God and stationed a guard" on the wall (Neh. 4:9). Nehemiah did both—prayed and went to work. It is not an "either/or" but a "both/and." God is sovereign, but He also calls men and women to be involved. Nehemiah gave God the glory for it all. After they completed the wall, they had a dedication and worship time to the Lord (Neh. 12:27–43). As a leader, you should celebrate the work God has done through your staff and volunteers. Dedications and celebrations are important. We want God, not simply us, to receive credit. We want to celebrate that God allowed us to be a part of what He is doing. Having a dedicated time to worship and be thankful is essential to any project. All glory to our great God!

What we can learn from Nehemiah in any endeavor that answers God's call:

- The power and importance of prayer.
- Any endeavor requires sacrifice from the leader—how far Nehemiah had to travel and all he sacrificed to be a part of what God was doing.
- Don't say "someone else can do it" when God is calling you to do it—don't make excuses.
- Attempt something big for God! It's better to have something not go as planned than to not be obedient. If you are obedient, you can never lose.
- It is amazing what God can do—never underestimate God!

Let's Be Bold

What often keeps us from building, investing, and growing? Well, we face the same challenges as every other generation of spiritual leaders: (1) We are overwhelmed with the demands of ministry already, so we can't add buildings or look for buildings on top of all the ministry we already do. (2) We spend so much time building our own houses that we don't have time or energy to build God's house as well. (3) We don't think we can do it. We know we need to be bolder and dream bigger, but the odds seem overwhelming. (4) We forget that we have an enemy who wars against us and wants us to stay small. Or (5) we have this fear of not being able to accomplish what God has given us to do, so we don't even try. We think God-sized assignments are only reserved for super Christians, so we don't step up to even attempt something big. However, when God gives you the vision, know that He will accomplish His will. His power is with you. And ultimately, it isn't about you being successful but about you being obedient.

The fact is, you can't do it all yourself. You need help. We all need help. Therefore, begin praying now for God to help you and for others to help you as well. I love how when they built the First and Second Temples, the entire community came together to accomplish the task.

Everyone worshiped God, and the legacy impacted generations. Even though where the Temple stood for close to a thousand years is the Dome of the Rock today, Jesus is still coming back through that Eastern Gate, and nobody will miss Him.

Part 4

Places

Physical & Online Spaces

Buildings are significant for every ministry. We are living in a time when we can do increasingly more online, and this is great. Many businesses are working to move in that direction. However, businesses are also still investing in bricks and mortar. From retail centers to office buildings, hotels, and sports coliseums, buildings are continuing to boom in the world today. And for the church and nonprofits, we, too, should be working to move more and more into the online space; however, for ministries there will still always be a need for buildings. Remember, ministry is about serving people. Therefore, buildings are significant for churches and nonprofits to have a place to gather, to meet physical needs, to serve others, to perform weddings, funerals, and food distribution, to have offices for staff and volunteers, and to increase ministry possibilities. Buildings are important for every ministry and yet are one of the biggest expenses. From buying a building to maintaining it, this is so important for every church, nonprofit, and organization to do right. I truly believe God provides for His people when it comes to building and properties. Buildings are important to God and to His people.

Chapter 7

MINISTRY IN
THE DIGITAL AGE

We are living in the digital age. Businesses, churches, non-profits, schools—everyone has realized this opportunity and need to be digital. Online services and Bible studies have exploded just as streaming services and online grocery shopping have. We were already headed this way, but the pandemic definitely sped up the process. We are living in what some have termed the "phygital"—physical and digital—age. Both are important. We must embrace the incredible opportunities that come with online engagement and yet continue to press into gathering in person with the body of Christ.

Online Matters

While buildings and physical space are a necessary part of effective ministry, more ministry opportunities are presenting themselves online. The physical building used to be the front door of the ministry, but now the website is an organization's front door. Investing in online ministry is essential for a church or nonprofit's future growth. This means the business of ministry includes apps, social media, online registration, payment tools, websites, and learning more about augmented reality and virtual reality. The ministries that embrace online and learn how to thrive in this space are the ones that will effectively impact lives and communities in the future.

People are watching more worship services online and engaging in ministries online as well. Churches and nonprofits need to be aware of their constituents' use of online resources, and we need to meet the needs of our growing online audiences as much as we are able. Online gives us the opportunity to reach the world. In fact, at Rolling Hills, we are seeing our online presence grow almost daily. Nearly every Sunday, we have someone raising their hand to accept Christ online. At JMI, this is how sponsors engage with the orphan or vulnerable child they have under their care, and get to be involved in ways that otherwise might be impossible if not for the digital space. Online is both now and the future. Churches and nonprofits need to be moving as much as we possibly can to be available online. And yet, for all the benefits and advantages of online ministry, we also need to continue to meet and minister to people in person.

Being In Person Matters

Live events still matter. Why? Because we know there is power in local community. And even though you can watch church online, it misses an opportunity to fellowship and worship in the presence of other believers. I love online church, but there is something special and powerful about being in person and physically present for the body of Christ. We were created for community—to live out the "one anothers." Even as our culture and society change, there will always be a need and desire for God's people to gather together.

It is not one or the other, but both. While digital spaces can help us reach a larger audience and are less expensive, we still need buildings for a physical space to gather and minister to people. There are creative ways for finding and using that physical space. We must be open to new ideas and ways to use the buildings God has entrusted to us more effectively and impactfully. Consider how our church buildings could be used during the rest of the week besides Sunday mornings to serve and meet the needs in our communities—whether it's to provide food, clothes, or even ESL training. It could be a preschool learning center during the mornings and host small group discipleship classes in the afternoon and care classes in the evenings.

Be Innovative

Land and buildings are expensive. But instead of giving up, this should cause us to be more innovative and creative. Churches have bought or leased former shopping malls, warehouses, and even mega sports stadiums and turned them into amazing church buildings that are impacting thousands of people for Christ. Some have even taken dead churches and redeemed those spaces.

I remember doing a mission trip and working with a church in Moscow that was meeting in an old Communist theater. Another church in the States had bought it for them, and they had done a great job of converting it into an amazing church building. There is much we can do with buildings overseas as we plant churches worldwide. Whether it is partnering with a church or nonprofit in another country or sponsoring missionaries on the ground, the money we have in the United States can go unbelievably far in some of the less resourced places in the world.

Raising Up the Next Generation

As churches and nonprofits, we must be intentional in raising up the next generation. From church on Sunday mornings to Christian school and after-school tutoring, buildings are significant for discipling the next generation. I am thankful I grew up in a church that invested heavily in the next generation. It had a gym, bowling alley, and skating rink. While those aren't necessary features in every church, their heart was to reach the next generation for Christ. Every church must think and plan for how to raise up the next generation through ministries for children and students. As culture tries to take religion out of the schools, it is incumbent upon parents and the church to invest in giving the next generation a spiritual foundation.

This is needed in big or small churches alike. Whether there is a volunteer (a teacher in a local school or someone with training) or paid staff, when you have educators who are trained to teach preschool, children's ministry, and student ministry, there are incredible benefits that occur. Every church should allocate some space for these programs. As Proverbs 22:6 says, "Teach a youth about the way he should go; even when he is old he will not depart from it." It is so important to start children off on the right path. It doesn't mean that they will not take some twists and turns in their life, but how they start is essential to their long-term spiritual health and growth. What we pass on matters. We are a link in the chain of passing on the Christian faith and values. What are our kids learning from us? We desperately need generational impact. The next generation needs to see us passionate about building God's church.

Remember, the Building Is Not the Vision

The goal of any ministry or church is transformation. Essentially, the goal is to see people helped, developed, and enriched. The heartbeat of a church or ministry is not about amassing more money and stuff. Resources and buildings can too easily become the goal in and of themselves. These are important, but they can never take the place of our ultimate goal in ministry—serving people. When we built our first building, a wise friend said, "The building is not the vision. The vision is the vision. The building is simply a tool to help us accomplish our God-given vision." So, how do we not let resources and buildings become the vision? This takes a lot of time, energy, and intentionality.

Buying Buildings and Property

Do you remember buying your first house? Do you remember how you stretched? I do. When I saw those numbers, I thought this was crazy. How could we ever repay this loan from the bank? I negotiated interest rates and sought wise advice, but at the end of the day, if we wanted the house, we needed to stretch, adjust our budget, and step out in faith. And boy, are we glad we did! We love our home and are so thankful to have raised our kids there. There have been so many memories and life changes. The same is true with a church home. You must pray, adjust your budget, and stretch.

Shortly after we had planted the church, I was on the campus of Belmont University. Dr. Gabhart was the longtime president of the university, and even though he was retired, he still went into the office on a part-time basis as President Emeritus. As I was walking across campus, Dr. Gabhart saw me. He was an active member of a local church and had heard about us starting Rolling Hills. He said, "Jeff, let me give you one piece of advice." I went over to him and waited with bated breath to hear this wisdom. He had led Belmont through many leadership challenges and periods of great growth. He was a man of character and integrity and was greatly respected by so many in Nashville. What was he going to say? What words of wisdom would he share with me? The anticipation was so intense. I waited for a moment, and then I responded, "Yes, Dr. Gabhart, I would love to hear your advice." He simply said, "Buy as much land as you can." That's it. Then he walked off.

I stood there trying to make sense of the encounter. What kind of advice was that? I needed something that would encourage me at that moment. But God knew. God knew what He was going to do. And God knew this was just the advice I needed to hear.

Here was a Christian university president who knew that it was not just about discipling students, but it was about building a university that would impact generations. Obviously, as a Christian university president, Dr. Gabhart was passionate about seeing students develop in Christ.

85

But he knew that there was more to overseeing a Christian university, or a church, than just the ministry side. The ministry is the essence, the why, but the business is what helps make that ministry happen. For all churches, private schools, and nonprofits, this is something we all must realize. The world has changed since I talked with Dr. Gabhart that day, but his advice still rings true. Three things hit me that day:

1. Land and buildings matter.
2. Always dream bigger.
3. Build to impact generations.

I believe we are at a particularly challenging time for sharing the gospel. So many people are online. And I believe this will continue to grow. So, yes—we need to be sharing the gospel online. But we must realize that ministry also happens in community. Living out the "one anothers" in community is important, which is why we must recognize our innate need for physical presence and not only focus on advancing in the digital space.

The apostle Paul went to cities because that is where most people lived. This is where a pastor, minister, Christian school, and nonprofit can have the most impact. However, it is becoming more of a challenge to find and buy land in major cities. Prices have increased so much that for many start-up churches, Christian schools, and nonprofits, land and buildings in cities are cost prohibitive. And many of the ministries and schools that did exist early on have sold their land and buildings and moved out.

Several years ago, I visited one of my good friends in New York City. We had a great weekend there, and as we walked all over the city—from my friend's high-rise apartment complex to his office, to lunches, dinners, and more—I noticed there were very few church buildings. There were lots of office buildings, fire stations, police precincts, parks, and stores, but very few churches, nonprofits, or private schools. So many people right here, I thought, and still there's such a need for sharing the gospel, meeting the needs of the underserved, raising up the next generation in godly morals and ethics, and developing community!

Now, I am thankful for the churches and ministries who *are* serving so faithfully in NYC and other cities. Keep going. What you do matters! My prayers are with you. I hope that we can encourage "each other, and all the more as you see the day drawing near" (Heb. 10:25).

Having a greater physical presence in communities and cities is a huge reason why understanding business principles matters. Yes, we can meet in homes, and so many churches do. This is great! Pray for the ministry to grow in homes. But many people point to the early church in Acts 2 and say that all churches should meet in homes. When you look at what Scripture says, it provides more context: "They devoted themselves to meeting together in the temple complex, and broke bread from house to house" (Acts 2:46). They did meet in homes, but they also met in the temple courts. They had three thousand people just from Pentecost! You can't put three thousand people in one home. They gathered for large group worship in the temple courts and then had small group gatherings in homes.

This is why churches built buildings, to be able to worship together in large groups. I don't believe that house church should be the end goal. It is great for small group settings—for more intimate gatherings where discipleship is lived out. But the large group gathering is important as well.

A Building Is a Tool to Accomplish God's Vision

So, how do we do it? In this crazy, expensive, challenging world, how do we build something that will outlast us for the glory of God? Well, we do three things: pray, ask others, and be creative.

We can lease and rent space, and we should—sometimes this is the most economical option. But we can also pray and ask for land and buildings to be used for God's purposes.

How many times do we skip prayer? Jesus said that faith the size of a mustard seed could move mountains, yet that this would not happen "except by prayer and fasting" (Matt. 17:20–21). And yet, we try everything else but prayer and fasting. We must learn to take our needs and concerns to God before anyone else. And after we have done that, we can look for opportunities the Lord may have placed in front of us. Ask people who own buildings to give them, lease them, or rent them out. Ask people to give money. Ask people to use their skills to join with you to build. Ask commercial real estate brokers, city and county governments, business owners . . . Seriously, all we have to do is ask! So often, we never ask. Pray, then do the work. God opens all kinds of doors, if we are just willing to be bold enough to ask.

We must learn to be creative. Jesus said we should be "as shrewd as serpents and as harmless as doves" (Matt. 10:16). Jesus encourages us that being wise is not simply using that wisdom for our own gain. We must learn how to be gentle in how we deal with people and love people, but be wise in our business and leadership endeavors. Being creative is using the wisdom God gave us for today's world. I remember Rick Warren saying, "Most churches build too small and too soon."[3] We serve a big God, so we need to dream bigger. We must think about not only where we are today, but where we could be tomorrow.

> *We must learn how to be gentle in how we deal with people and love people, but be wise in our business and leadership endeavors.*

The problem is not money. How many times have we said, "If we just had more money," or "I would do this if I just had money"? Remember,

Jesus sent out the seventy-two and told them to take nothing with them (Luke 10:1–4). But the power of God was with them, and this same God is with you.

We live in the wealthiest nation that has ever existed in history! We also live at the wealthiest time in history. And we serve a God who holds all the riches of the world in His hands. There is all the money in the world all around us. The issue is how we most effectively use the money God has entrusted to us and how we cast vision for others to join and invest in God's work.

Chapter 8

THE 5 Rs OF MINISTRY BUILDINGS

There are 5 Rs—Reclaim, Reimagine, Revitalize, Restore, and Revival—that are important for every ministry, both now and in the future. Let's dive into each one and see how God is giving us the opportunity to make a significant difference for His glory today.

Reclaim

The word for this time in the history of the church is *reclaim*. Reclaim the faith. Reclaim passion. Reclaim the vision. And reclaim the buildings—there are a lot of church buildings out there already standing ready to be filled with the people of God worshiping Him. Let's reclaim old church buildings and bring them back to life with the Spirit and power of our God. There are so many church buildings in cities that have been built generations before us. What if we could reclaim these buildings in the name of Jesus?

Instead of older church congregations simply selling their buildings and then the building being gone forever, what if we could begin to reclaim these buildings for the glory of God? So many older churches, as their congregation becomes older, believe the only option is to sell their building to meet their financial obligations. But then the church building, the sacred space, is gone. It becomes a condo building, an office complex, or even a shopping center.

One of my good friends tells the story of driving by this older church, and when he drove by the next week it was a Hindu temple. Another church building in our city is now a bar. This was never the congregation's dream. They wanted to do something that would impact generations for Christ, and yet they couldn't see another way. And the crazy part about this is that since a church is legally a 501(c)(3), the money has to be donated to another ministry. While this is fine in the short run, it leaves a bigger hole in the community in the long run.

What if this could be reimagined? What if selling the building is not the only option?

What if the church building could be reclaimed by joining together with another congregation, a younger church plant, or a vibrant church that is operating multiple campuses? What a win for everyone and especially for the kingdom. We must learn to put aside denominational differences and work together, even reaching into smaller communities that have a great building in the center of town to reach the community.

Our church first started in an apartment clubhouse. Then we met in a hotel ballroom. There were even times when we couldn't meet at the hotel so we met in a bridal shop or a barn. The building our church was able to buy was built as a warehouse.

There are buildings all around us that we can reclaim and use for God's glory. When we launched our first multisite campus nine years ago, we started in a school in South Nashville. It worked well, even though there was setup and tear-down each week, but it came equipped with a school auditorium and obviously classrooms and—this is a big one—parking. All of these are important, and being in a school worked out great for a while.

We were renting the school, and we knew we couldn't be there long-term. So, we kept praying on where to go next. Then another school opened in a new booming area. We knew God was calling us to this area for the long term, so we made the move over to this new community. Meeting in a school puts you right in the middle of the community you are trying to reach. Everyone knows where the local school is, so it makes it easy to share with others. We met there for five years, and God continued to grow His church.

Again, we knew we needed to go somewhere else. But land and buildings in this community were so expensive. So, we began praying for a miracle. We launched a capital campaign called "For the Kingdom," and we asked our entire church community to pray and give. We didn't know where, but we knew God had a plan and He was leading us to the next place to reclaim for His glory.

This time it was a church building. There was a small church in the center of the community that was on the decline. They had about twenty to thirty people who were all passionate and dedicated servants of Jesus, but there was not any momentum or growth. They were having to make hard decisions about what to do with the building. Maintenance and repair costs were adding up. As we began talking with them, it became abundantly clear to both groups that God was calling us to work together.

The church voted to join with us, and now we had a building and land in a prime spot in the middle of the community. It was truly a miracle. And now the church had more people to help with the ministry, the outreach, and the maintenance of the building. While the existing building was small, it did provide a place to meet and grow until we could take the next step.

Church buildings are already there. They simply need to be reclaimed and used for the glory of God. It may take some money to renovate and update, but this is a lot less money than building from the ground up. Also, the property is already zoned for a church. Many times, new locations cannot be rezoned.

Many of these church buildings are in prime locations already. To buy the real estate alone would take exponential dollars. Now, the money from those in the congregation can be used to renovate the building and for ministry and missions.

Church Mergers

One of the most remarkable trends in ministry today is the use of shared space and even church mergers. When an older, dying congregation realizes they are sitting on a valuable asset, instead of selling that asset and giving the proceeds to a different cause, they begin to partner with another church. For a newer church plant or a multisite location, it is often too expensive to try to buy a building or to buy land and build from the ground up. The two churches can then join together in a new and more effective way to reach the community for Christ. I have been a part of multiple church mergers with incredible success. The beauty is seeing an older, even dying church gain new life and thrive! People in that community are being reached and served with the gospel, and lives are being changed. There are some definite ways to do this well, and this can be such a great option for churches and nonprofits at all stages of their life cycle.

The Call

As our main campus in Franklin continued to grow, we began to pray about planting a church campus in Nashville. People were moving to Nashville in record numbers (and still are), and we felt God leading us to plant a campus that would reach new people for Christ and impact the community. Again, property values in Nashville were skyrocketing and we were having a difficult time finding a location big enough to even rent.

With three of my closest friends in ministry, I spent one day praying and looking for places. We could not find anything that worked, so we were a little discouraged. I began driving back from Nashville when my phone buzzed. It was John Garner. I knew John, but we weren't close.

John had served for years as the leader of Recreation Ministry at Life-Way. I had heard he was now pastoring a church, but we had never connected on this. And now he was calling me!

John began to tell me that he was pastoring an older congregation called Belmont Heights Baptist Church near Belmont University's campus in Nashville. He said, "Jeff, we are an older congregation, and we used to be one of the biggest churches in the city. But now we are not reaching the younger generation. Can we get together, and you help me learn how to reach college students and young adults?" I sat speechless. He didn't even know I was driving back from looking for locations. This was completely a divine appointment. I responded, "Of course, I would love to get together. Let's meet for lunch as soon as you can."

At this first lunch, we talked about what God was doing at Belmont Heights and Rolling Hills. I remember John's humility and faithfulness to God. He truly wanted to reach the next generation for Christ, and so was willing to do whatever it would take. This began a yearlong journey of seeing Belmont Heights become our Rolling Hills Nashville campus. There were major challenges to overcome, but God was faithful all along the way.

I'm so thankful for the amazing godly saints who were at Belmont Heights. They sacrificed, paid for, and built beautiful buildings over the years for the glory of our great God. Yet, as times have changed, they were not able to meet the needs of the community around them. Cities and communities may change, but the gospel never does. We must be willing to take new approaches if we are to reach and engage people through the changing times.

We launched the new Nashville campus at Belmont Heights, and instantly saw college students and young families from the neighborhood come. The people of Belmont Heights were so excited! God was answering their prayers as well as ours. We were all coming together to make a difference for His glory.

As exciting as this was, there was one major challenge. Years ago,

Belmont Heights had sold their building to Belmont University. So, essentially, the church building had a limited time. Belmont is a great university, and it was (and still is) growing quickly. They needed the space, and therefore we again needed a new place. But this time I had more faith that God would provide.

The first time we were looking for a location for the Nashville campus, a friend had given me the name of the pastor of Park Avenue Baptist Church. Patrick Hamilton is a great man of God with a missional heart. Patrick was younger, but the congregation was older. The church was large in the past, but the demographic had changed, and they were not reaching the people around them. I had called Patrick before, but we had not connected.

Some time later, I reached out to Patrick again. I came to find out later from Patrick that he was nervous to return my phone call because he did not know what that would mean. But I so love and appreciate Patrick's faith because he said he finally came to the point where he prayed, "God, this is Your church and not my church. I willingly submit to Your will. I trust You." Patrick called me back, and we met for lunch. This started an incredible journey.

I will never forget going to the meeting with the leaders of Park Avenue. That first night we gathered in a room with about twenty of the deacons and ministry leaders. We shared what God was doing at Rolling Hills, and they shared about what God had done in the past at Park Avenue and how they had been praying for Him to do a new work today. Some expressed fear and concern about joining together with another church, but they realized they needed to do some things differently if they were to impact their community for Christ. There were some tense moments as people shared their worries and emotions. The authenticity was palpable. These brothers and sisters in Christ truly loved their church. I sat there unsure which way the meeting would go—some were in favor of joining together and others were hesitant. This is when it all changed.

One of the deacons of Park Avenue is a man named Raymond

Kuzunsi. Raymond and his wife, Gigi, were immigrants from Congo. They had literally walked out of their country with only their small children. They made their way to Nashville and Park Avenue Baptist Church years ago. Raymond motioned that he was going to say something, and the room became silent. I didn't know what he was going to say, but I knew this was a God moment.

He said, "Friends, I know we all have a lot of emotion right now. As a church, we have been praying for years that God would answer our prayers and grow His church. We have all worked so hard, and we are tired. We need help. We can't do it all. I am reminded of the story in Acts 12 when the church was gathered together to pray for Peter, who was in prison. God answered their prayers and an angel led Peter past the guards and out of the jail. Peter came to the house where the church was praying, and he knocked on the door. Remember the servant girl answering the door? She couldn't believe it was Peter, so she closed the door. Let's not close the door when our God is obviously doing a miracle."

That was it. That was the moment the Holy Spirit brought us all together, and we have seen God do so much. As Pastor Patrick says, "Now we are seeing baptisms! Now we are hearing babies. Now we are seeing weddings. It is what we all prayed for all those years. God answered our prayers."

I love seeing this. The joining together of congregations and, through the work of God, making a difference. This is what we are all called to do. We must always remember that we are simply servants of God. All of this is His. He is the One we serve. Our God is the One who changes lives for His glory.

The Cambodian Congregation

One of the most amazing and unexpected parts of the joining together of Rolling Hills and Park Avenue is that Park Avenue had a Cambodian congregation meeting in their facility. Pastor Khem Sam had been pastoring the congregation for over thirty years. When I heard

Pastor Khem's story, I was literally moved to tears. He accepted Christ in a refugee camp coming out of the killing fields. God spared him and his family, and he dedicated his life to serving Jesus, his Savior. This opened my eyes to the need of providing space for international congregations.

So often, our church buildings in the United States sit empty six days a week. This is not good stewardship. If God has entrusted a building to your church or nonprofit, then "fill it up and wear it out." The Cambodian congregation has inspired us to do more, and I am so thankful for Pastor Khem Sam, who models Jesus and who continues to impact his own people with the gospel.

Reimagine

Start to see every place as an opportunity to further God's kingdom. Learn to reimagine everything you see as a place to be used for God's glory. Think about your home as a place to adopt or foster children, and the homes of those in your congregation or ministry as places for church services, ministry areas, office space, or even distribution centers. Start seeing schools as places to minister to the needs of children and families in your community and places to host a church plant or a multisite congregation. See and imagine older, dying churches as buildings to be reimagined and reenergized in order to reach your community for Christ. Be bold and be creative.

Learn to reimagine everything you see as a place to be used for God's glory.

What if your existing building could be reimagined with leases in part of the building to help meet financial needs? Lease out unused space and keep space for church services, children's ministry, and more. Share parking, or rent out the church's parking during the week to make extra income for ministries.

What if your building or a building in your community could be reimagined to be a private Christian school? Imagine your building filled with children learning and growing in Jesus throughout the week. You can even join with another organization to run the school, but just start to reimagine the space being used to raise up the next generation in Christ. You would be giving kids a spiritual foundation that will last a lifetime.

What if the church property could be reimagined to include a ministry center—with food, clothes, housing for the homeless, church services on Sunday mornings, and ministry throughout the week? What if churches partnered with local nonprofits to meet the needs of those in the community every day of the week?

What if your building could host international congregations for worship? Either on Sunday mornings in a different part of the building or at a different time in the week. So many neighborhoods have changed. Different cultural groups have moved into different areas of cities. Sometimes churches find themselves in a changing area, but now they have the unique opportunity to truly impact the people around them as well as those driving to the church. These may be small congregations, but they are growing and reaching very specific groups.

Recently, we were able to join with a local church in the Nashville area. This church had been hosting three different international congregations. The church has a Congolese congregation and a Burmese congregation. They have been meeting there for several years at a reduced rental rate, but now these two congregations are larger than the parent church congregation. This is so awesome to see the impact for the kingdom!

Let's reimagine how and where we do church.

Renew Church

Several years ago, I was talking with one of my dearest friends who was a pastor of a mainline denominational church. This pastor had served faithfully at this church for many years. However, he had begun to feel God's call to plant a new church. While the existing church was doing fine (financially it was meeting weekly expenses), their attendance was on a downward trend. It was not in dire straits yet, but it was not growing or reaching the community around them. This pastor began to reimagine church in a way that would reach the community.

We've all been there. You have spent countless hours and maybe even sleepless nights reimagining church or ministry in a given area. God has stirred something in you that has called you to more. Now, maybe you can do that in your existing situation. Maybe you have the freedom to steer your current church or nonprofit in a more effective and life-impacting way. Keep praying and dreaming and be ready when God calls you to take that step.

After meeting with my pastor friend, we prayed for God's direction and timing in the reimagining stage. Then, one day, God made it very clear, and praise God for my friend's boldness, because when the "call" came, he took the step of faith.

How do you know when it is God's timing? Here are a few ways:

- The power of the Holy Spirit—many times God speaks through His still, small voice (1 Kings 19:12) that reverberates in our heart and soul.
- A change in circumstances—sometimes God has to push His kids, like a bird has to push her babies, out of the nest.
- An unbelievable opportunity—some things are just too good to be true. Sometimes we dismiss it because we can't believe it, but God still does work miracles.
- The wisdom of godly people in our lives—God speaks through another Christ follower directly to us.

The timing will never be perfect—that is why it is called faith. We must trust and believe.

My friend had been watching what God was doing at Rolling Hills from the very beginning. He had prayed with us and for us. For years, I had wanted him to come be on our staff team. Yet God had other plans. He was already invested in his own church community, and he was the one to reach the people there for Jesus.

When God's call came, he stepped out in faith and left this pastor job with the salary, benefits, and comforts to follow God into the unknown. I have so much respect for church planters. They are bold. They love Jesus and truly want to make a difference for His glory.

By God's grace, there were twelve families in the community (not just at that church) who had the same call and desire to be a part of a reimagined church. These twelve couples all booked airline tickets and flew out to Nashville to spend a weekend with our leadership team to talk about planting what would come to be known as Renew Church in Waco, Texas. The weekend was unbelievable. It was a time of praying, dreaming, planning, and believing God's best for His church. We all knew we were a part of something special.

Along with any other aspect of ministry, there is a lot of "business" involved in church planting. This is why for church plants it is important to have a "sponsoring" church or nonprofit. From setting up the new church's 501(c)(3) to writing bylaws, renting places to meet, creating a website, giving tax deductions for charitable donations, setting up bank accounts, buying the right sound equipment, paying for children's curriculum, obtaining a CCLI license for the worship songs you sing . . . and the list goes on and on. You need someone to help with all the business logistics. The same is true in starting a nonprofit. This is why a "sponsoring church," a church consultant, or a ministry coach is so important.

It was great to work with Renew to help them through this setup stage and allow people to start giving immediately through our business office at Rolling Hills. This helped provide money for renting buildings, paying staff, and buying supplies. People who gave were also able to receive tax deductions for their charitable contributions. Having all the "business" in place early on allowed the "ministry" to flourish.

Renew Church was born. And God began to do miracles. There was a local church with a small private school in the area, but the church was struggling to reach the community and to pay the bills. My friend went and had a conversation with the existing pastor, and they decided to reimagine what church in the area could look like. They were so creative that the older, existing church would meet at 8 a.m., and Renew would have services at 9:30 a.m. and 11 a.m. They would share the expenses on the building. This worked well.

Within a year, the older pastor, who was planning on retiring, asked my friend to pastor both congregations and bring the two churches together. They prayed, voted, and moved forward. Now, in only three years, there are over a thousand people attending Renew Church, and God is doing a great work there. Pastor Wayne is an incredible man of God, and a true pastor. He loves people well and makes such an impact for Christ in the Waco community.

The Russian Church in Moldova

A few years ago, I visited the largest Russian-speaking church in Moldova. It's in a big, beautiful building. I asked one of our staff team members to tell me the story of the church. She said that during Communism, the church had to go underground. Many of the pastors and lay leaders were put in jail for their faith, and some were even killed. Yet there was a group of Christ followers in Chisinau who would meet underground together and worship and who believed that God would impact their community.

This group of believers went to the government to ask permission to build a church building. They had to be licensed by the government and this meant Communist leaders would come into their services. They would receive the same answer no every time, sometimes even being beaten or sentenced to jail time, but the underground church leaders believed this was what God was calling them to do. They kept asking.

Then one day they asked, and with sarcasm the government leader said, "You can have the trash dump outside the city to build your church." The trash dump. But the church leaders rejoiced. They went back to their underground church and told them the good news. They all rejoiced that the Lord had heard their prayers and went to work. Every day after their jobs, they would go to the trash dump and begin to move trash with their bare hands. They would work through the night clearing the land. When they began to build, they were mocked and ridiculed, but they kept going. It took them many years, even generations, of working together.

And by God's grace and in His timing, they completed the work a few years before Communism fell. Today, the church is thriving. The growth of Chisinau meant that the city grew around the church, so the church now sits in the heart of the city, and attendance is booming—only God!

The Sunday morning I was there, I was blown away by how many people gathered. The place was packed with people of all ages—from precious babies and children to teenagers, young adults, and older adults. Many of our Justice & Mercy International staff attend this church in Chisinau, Moldova. That morning, many people were baptized. We also shared the Lord's Supper, and I sat with tears in my eyes. It was so awesome to feel the Spirit of the Lord and to see what He was doing in the lives of so many.

Can you imagine those Christ followers in heaven today, that "large cloud of witnesses" (Heb. 12:1) rejoicing and celebrating as they are seeing their great-grandkids, their great-great-grandkids, and their entire community worshiping Jesus? Their sacrifice and commitment to Christ is truly impacting generations for the glory of God!

Revitalize

The Ryman

In the heart of downtown Nashville is the iconic Ryman Theater. Everyone who is anyone in music has performed (or wanted to perform) at the Ryman. It is the home of country music and the heartbeat of "Music City." It is an amazing place, and I encourage you to come to the Ryman and hear some music one day.

Did you know that the Ryman was actually built as a church? That's right. It is called the "Mother Church." In 1885, an evangelist named Sam Jones was hosting a tent revival about three blocks away from where the Ryman now sits. On one of the nights, a riverboat captain named Thomas Ryman came to the revival and gave his life to Christ. He was so compelled by the gospel that he asked Sam Jones what they could do together to impact Nashville for Christ. And that is how the Ryman was born.

Thomas Ryman was a wealthy business owner. When he joined Sam Jones in the ministry of the gospel, together they felt God leading them to build the Ryman as a church—a gospel tabernacle. And that is what they did. In 1892, the first worship service was held there. And still today, 130 years later, the Ryman sits at the heart of Nashville. While the vision and mission for the Ryman have changed over the years, you can still feel the presence of God in the place. From the pews to the gift of music, God's presence still resides there. What are we building in our day and in our generation that will long outlast us and bring glory to God for generations? That is the question that we all must ask ourselves.

The church brings light to the community. What if we could see communities revitalized with the Spirit of God? What if we could go into downtown metropolitan cities and even rural communities and begin to revitalize there? How amazing to work with a developer to transform an old church building or an old warehouse, shopping center, or office building into a thriving place of worship and ministry.

Haywood Hills

Recently, we merged with an older church in a community that had changed around them. This church used to be large and thriving. Their building has a commercial kitchen and a gymnasium, along with a chapel, a worship center, adult classrooms, and a wonderful kids' space. But the attendance had dwindled since most of the people who attend there have moved farther out from where the church is located.

The area is filled with so many people from different nationalities. It is a beautiful mixing of people speaking many different languages and coming from countries all over the world. What an incredible opportunity of God bringing the world to us.

God has blessed us with the opportunity to bring light to the community. To boldly preach and teach the world about God. To offer weekly programming for children and families. To host community events to bring everyone together.

Eugene Peterson writes that there are "times in our lives when repairing the building where we worship is an act of obedience every bit as important as praying in that place of worship."[4]

In a world of fear and struggle, what if the church could be a place that offers joy, life, and freedom? The church brings beauty, hope, and life into the hearts of neighborhoods and communities all over the world.

The Impact of Multisite

Having multiple campuses is like having children. The first commandment that the Jews see in the Hebrew Bible is to "be fruitful, multiply, fill the earth, and subdue it" (Gen. 1:28). To reproduce is of the Lord. Healthy churches need to reproduce. We need to be planting other churches and having multiple campuses. Both are important. When you have babies, you invest a lot of money, time, and energy in them, and then you watch them grow. This is the joy and beauty of parenting.

Your dream is that they outgrow you. That they grow and flourish and impact the world in a greater way than you ever did or could. This is healthy. Every church should be thinking and praying about how to launch a church plant or another campus. Just like children, it is worth the investment. This is how you revitalize communities and cities as well as revitalize your own congregation.

Recently, we were meeting with a church about a potential merger. Patrick Hamilton, who had been the Senior Pastor at Park Avenue Church when we merged with them, stood up in front of the Haywood Hills congregation to share his story of merging with Rolling Hills. Patrick said, "At first, I was scared. I didn't know how this would go. But I trusted that God had a plan. Our church was dying. I was working endless hours to try to grow, and we simply were not reaching the community around us. Something had to give because I was about to burn out and our church was about to close." It was silent in the room because this was the current story at Haywood Hills as well. It was an older congregation, and they were tired. They were amazing saints of God but simply worn out with being older and having no young people in the church. They weren't seeing any growth.

Patrick continued. "I must tell you all. This merger with Rolling Hills has been the best thing that has ever happened to me, to my family, and to our church at Park Avenue. In fact, I don't think I would still be in ministry today if it had not been for the merger with Rolling Hills. I feel like the weight is lifted, and I can be a husband and father again as well as continue to pastor. Our church campus is now growing. We are seeing babies in the nursery. We are seeing baptisms, people committing their lives to Jesus. There is joy and life in the place again. We are so thankful. This has been the answer to our prayers." What a testimony to what God can do through adoptions and mergers.

Now, church mergers and adoptions are not perfect. There are challenges. Just like in marriage, there is a time of adjustment. Just like having a baby, it costs a lot of money, time, and energy, but it is all worth it. Because of the love and the calling, you work through the challenges. And you are not working alone, but working together. With adopting or merging with older buildings comes the cost of maintenance. This is why it is such a struggle for aging congregations. Together, you can tackle these challenges and return the focus to reaching the community for Christ and growing His church.

God says, "I am making everything new" (Rev. 21:5). Focus on what you do have and not on what you don't have. We didn't have any money, staff, or a building. But we did have, and still do have, a very big God! The same power that raised Jesus from the dead is alive in you. The power that was available to the early church is the same power that is available to you. We serve a God of miracles who is passionate about building His church. "Unless the LORD builds a house, its builders labor over it in vain" (Ps. 127:1). It doesn't matter if your church, nonprofit, or ministry is in a physical building or online—if God is not present, then you will not succeed. You have a heavenly Father who loves you and who called you to this—allow Him to build His house!

Restore

We must restore for the "common good." From Jewish synagogues to early churches in America, places of worship have always been at the center of a community for worship, schools, weddings, and funerals. People and communities looked to these places. What if we could restore the common good? What if we could take and use the buildings that are already there? Yes, reclaim church buildings for worship, but also for the common good. Maybe even warehouses, office buildings, and apartment complexes can be restored to become places of ministry and hope. Churches and nonprofit centers can become places to vote, host school graduations, and even hold first responder trainings. By partnering with city, state, and national government agencies, other nonprofits, and even other churches, we can redeem and restore for the common good.

There are a few churches who have partnered with local government agencies to create what is known as "Dream Centers." These are remarkable places to restore cities and communities. By providing services from food and clothes distribution to ESL and financial counseling, these centers are radically transforming communities.

There are three ministries that we have partnered with who are doing this in our city and community. First, let me tell you about 4:13Strong. This nonprofit organization was started by a man in our church, Steve Norris. Steve was a successful businessman who retired early. He knew God had a greater plan for his life, so he began to pray about the next step in his spiritual journey. When Steve and I were talking one day, he began to tell me about his heart for young men who have had a rough start in life. Young men who grew up in a tough part of town, who have maybe been to jail, but who just needed help and a fresh start. He longed to help restore men and raise up spiritual leaders.

Steve started 4:13Strong based on Philippians 4:13: "I am able to do all things through [Christ] who strengthens me." Today, Steve is making an incredible difference. The state of Tennessee has allowed him to use dormitories for housing these young men. Every quarter, he takes a new class through physical, mental, and spiritual development. Steve uses our Nashville campus as home base for his 90-Day Challenge, and the guys are involved in church on Sundays. Then, at the end of the ninety days, Steve has partnered with local businesses to help these men get jobs. This is truly impacting their lives, their families, and the entire city.

Then, there is Paul Schmitz. Paul was a businessman, but his heart was broken over the homelessness in Nashville. As Paul and I were talking and praying one day, he commented that he would love to leave his job and do something to help the homeless. By God's grace, and Paul's faith, he took that next step in his spiritual journey to make a difference in the name of Jesus. Paul partnered with an amazing local business, Lee Company, to build mobile showers. He parks the shower trucks at the church, and then with groups of volunteers goes to downtown Nashville to give the homeless showers, haircuts, and hygiene products. This has helped many be able to go for job interviews and find places to live. Paul shares the love of Jesus, and God is now using what Paul started, ShowerUp, in many cities across the country.

Also, there is Margaret Jane. Margaret Jane was a stay-at-home mom when God broke her heart for the needs in our community. Franklin Estates is the most under-resourced and underserved area in Franklin. As a church, we had been working in this area with a ministry called Path United. Margaret Jane stepped out and began to lead this ministry, which offers after-school tutoring to children and students. And what a difference God has made in the lives of many through this ministry. She is truly restoring hope and life to this area and to so many families.

As churches and nonprofits, we have this incredible opportunity to do something significant in our community for the glory of our great God. It has been said that "a man may do an immense deal of good, if he does not care who gets the credit for it."[5] As we pray and partner with other churches, nonprofits, and ministries, God can use His people to do a mighty work for His glory. We can restore our communities and cities and impact countless lives for Him. There is such power and beauty in the ministry of restoration—from hearts to marriages to families and even communities. This is God's specialty and His calling for all of us as His disciples today.

The Church in Moscow

Several years ago, I was in Moscow on a mission trip. We went to this beautiful Christian church that was meeting in an old Communist theater. I asked them to tell me the story. Some of the leaders recalled how they were a small church meeting underground during the Communist regime. Many of their pastors and leaders in the church had spent time in jail for their faith. Others were sent off to Siberia and were never heard from again. My heart broke for the persecution that our brothers and sisters in Christ have endured for the gospel.

After the fall of Communism in Russia, they had this new freedom. But they did not have any money. Then, they said, some church in the

States was moved by God to help restore Christianity in Russia, so they heard about the church and gave them $2 million to build a church in Moscow. This Communist theater became available, and they bought it—for $2 million. Today, it is a thriving church community. Jesus is being preached and lives saved in a place built under a regime that tried to do away with God. Our mission team led Bible clubs there with hundreds of children and students, and then revival services at night. The irony was not lost on me: from a former Communist theater to a thriving church. God redeeming and restoring.

I know there are amazing companies like Hobby Lobby who want to help restore communities and are partnering with churches and nonprofits. I am so thankful for Christian-owned businesses like Hobby Lobby, Chick-fil-A, and more. I continue to pray for other Christ-centered companies to catch a vision for making a difference in their communities, our nation, and our world. Think about how much money God has entrusted to some of these American companies. It is staggering. And here's the incredible part—if companies invest in churches in their communities, then the entire community gets stronger. You then have healthier employees, higher morale, and better working conditions. Everyone wins. Less crime and more progress. Less violence and more peace. This is how businesses, churches, nonprofits, and schools can work together to change communities and our nation.

Revival

There was recently a revival that took place at Asbury College that captured the nation. Seeing the pictures and the videos was inspiring. The revival started when college students spontaneously stayed in Hughes Auditorium following a regularly scheduled chapel service on February 8, 2023. The revival continued for over two weeks, with people coming from all over the country to gather in the auditorium to pray, worship, and be together in the presence of God. Many students committed or recommitted their lives to Jesus. And from this, other revivals began to take place on college campuses across the nation.

As I watched this, I thanked God for showing up in such a powerful way, and I also thought about all those who had gone before those college students and had given money, worked, and invested in building Hughes Auditorium on that campus. Many of them were watching from heaven and rejoicing. They knew God was going to do something big in the next generation, and they invested in what would truly matter. I'm so thankful for the faithful servants who have gone before us who have built these auditoriums, chapels, church buildings, food pantries, clothes closets, and ministry centers. We stand today on the shoulders of those who have gone before us, and God used them in their day to help prepare for revival in our day.

Our prayer is for revival to sweep across our nation, on every college campus, and in the great halls of our state and country. We pray for revival to come to our families, our communities, our nation, and our world. We are in desperate need. *This is Your time, so come, Lord Jesus!*

Revivals are short-term and in a specific place. They impact a group of people and draw their hearts back to the heart of God. These are reset moments for churches and institutions. Revivals also lead to Great Awakenings. There have been four Great Awakenings in the history of the United States (some would say five with the Jesus Revolution of the '60s and '70s). Each Great Awakening has started with a revival, as a group of Christ followers gather in a building to pray. I truly believe the next great spiritual awakening is coming soon. Many times, these come after major events in our nation—wars, economic crises, or global events. We could be seeing the next Great Awakening in our lifetime, and we could be a part of it! What if we all began gathering to radically pray for God's presence and healing over our community, city, nation, and world? Imagine what God can and will do. And we can be in the front row, seeing it all.

What people need today is not more politics. We have been consumed with politics, and yet we struggle in so many places. What the world doesn't need is more technology. We have more technology than ever, and yet our lives are more complicated and stressful than ever. What the world doesn't need is more distractions and entertainment. We have more streaming channels, games, concerts, sports, and events than ever, and yet it is never enough. What our world needs is Jesus. And Jesus is truly the Hope of every life. The church is the vehicle for bringing Christ Jesus to people today. This is our opportunity. Let's not miss it! May the Lord bring revival and a great spiritual awakening today. And may He start with us.

Part 5

Position

Brand Identity & Kingdom Impact

One of Jesus' most famous parables is the parable of the talents (Matt. 25:14–30). This is such a strong parable in which Jesus shows that we all have a responsibility, regardless of how little or how much He has given into our care. Every one of us has been entrusted with time, money, resources, abilities, and opportunities by the Master Himself. How will we use what has been entrusted to us? Will we be bold and invest it all for the glory of God, or will we live in fear and bury what He has entrusted to us? If we are wise, we will be given more, but if we are lazy, then we will lose whatever we have. We know that our God is a God of grace and mercy, but that still doesn't excuse us from doing our best. We must never be lazy, but must take the time to do the work. Let's learn as much as we can and invest it all for building God's kingdom.

Chapter 9

DEVELOP A PLAN
FOR MINISTRY

The first year we started as a church, we did not have a lot. A few people and no building, staff, or money, but we knew it couldn't be just about us. It was an exciting time, but we knew we wanted to make a difference. A friend of mine from a nonprofit ministry in Texas called me and asked if we could take a mission trip to Moldova. I replied, "Where's Moldova?" He went on to tell me that Moldova is the poorest and smallest country in the former Soviet Union. It sits between Romania and Ukraine (with the war in Ukraine today, everyone now knows where Moldova is located). My heart broke when he said, "And 60 percent of girls trafficked into prostitution in Eastern Europe come out of this country of four million." Even though our church was small, I knew we had to do something.

Eight months after starting the Bible study, we took eighteen people and went on our first mission trip to Moldova. We worked with orphaned and vulnerable children at an old Communist campground. During the summers, they take the kids from the orphanages who have no place to go—no grandparents, aunts, uncles, friends, or teachers to stay with—and put them in a campground for the summer so they can do work on the orphanages. At that campground, the kids slept two to a single bed. They each had one pair of shoes, shorts, and one shirt. They had simple meals with bread and soup. Their toilets were holes in the ground. And they had really nothing to do.

We came to Internat 2 and discovered the most beautiful and amazing children. When we walked in, there were about two hundred kids so excited to see an American for the first time. They were in shock, and we felt our hearts being filled with God's love. We brought crafts, games, and Bible stories to share. The kids loved it. After a week of being there, we stood in a sunflower field and prayed for God to show us how to take care of these precious children, and so many others like them in Moldova, going forward.

We came home and began to pray and plan for how to do more. We built the work in Moldova into our church budget, and we scheduled a three-day strategic planning retreat to pray and plan how we could ultimately impact the entire country with the love of Jesus. We knew it was a God-sized call, but these children were now in our hearts and a part of our family. This is what God was calling us to do and be as His church. We put big Post-it notes on the wall, prayed and fasted, and began writing down plans for what God wanted us to do to impact every orphan and vulnerable child in Moldova. Ideas and dreams kept coming. We would brainstorm, back up, and start to create a plan for how to get there. We had a lot of other things to do at the time just to keep the young church going, but we knew we needed this sacred time to set the course for making an impact in the lives of these children we love.

After returning from that first trip to Moldova and having our strategic planning time to pray and dream about how we could impact all the children and the entire country for Christ, we made a commitment as a church to follow that strategic plan and begin to take the next steps for accomplishing what God had put on our hearts to do—impact an entire country for Christ and minister to every orphan and vulnerable child in

Moldova. It seemed overwhelming, but we knew God would help us to carry out His assignment. We started by doing two mission trips the next year and then three the following year. The ministry in Moldova began to grow, and we were taking forty to fifty people annually to serve there after only three years.

Then, as people became mobilized and passionate, we began to address the major problem of children having to leave the state-run orphanages at the age of fifteen. This is where they were so susceptible to human trafficking for the girls and organized crime for the boys. They had to survive somehow, or they would end up on the streets. The sad truth was that many were not surviving at that time. Can you imagine being fifteen years old and not having any place to go? Can you imagine being on the streets with nothing? That is what was happening. These kids are smart, beautiful, and full of potential, but they were not surviving after the age of fifteen, and we had to do something about it.

This is when we as a church decided to buy a Transitional Living Home in Moldova for kids to live in after they had to leave the orphanage. We began to meet, pray, and plan how to accomplish this. And the idea of starting our own nonprofit, called Justice & Mercy International, was born. Through JMI, we have seen God do an incredible work in Moldova. There is still so much more to do, but we never could have dreamed what God would accomplish. I will always think back to that strategic planning time following that first mission trip to Moldova as the beginning of God's plan to help us impact an entire country for Christ.

There is a great exchange between Alice and the Cheshire Cat in Lewis Carroll's *Alice in Wonderland*:

"Would you tell me, please, which way I ought to go from here?"
"That depends a good deal on where you want to get to," said the Cat.
"I don't much care where—" said Alice.
"Then it doesn't matter which way you go," said the Cat.[6]

For every leader and every organization, it is important to identify the calling and then determine a plan to accomplish that call. Ministries and churches should be the best-run organizations in the world because we have eternal implications at stake. Google, Amazon, or McDonald's may run a great business, but ultimately, what they are doing will not last. There will be new trends, new businesses, but the Word of the Lord stands forever. People can make a lot of money, but no one can take it with them. In churches and ministries, we are transforming lives for the glory of God. This is eternal! We have an incredible calling, and we need to do it right and do it well. You must have a plan and know where you are going. As the old saying goes, "If you fail to plan, you plan to fail." If you are walking with the Lord, then you can never fail spiritually. However, if you do spend the time planning and seeking God's wisdom and direction, then you can accomplish far more for His glory.

Developing a Strategic Plan

Every ministry and organization started for a purpose. It's critical to keep that purpose before the people in the organization by constantly telling the stories of ministry and success. However, the danger is that the calling and the vision can become lost over time. People, even the leader, can find themselves doing a lot of work that may or may not actually be leading the organization toward the desired objective.

When we first launched Rolling Hills, we had a small group of us that met with a man in our church who was a business consultant. He did strategic planning for companies, and I asked him if he could help us as we were setting the direction for this young church. He agreed, and we spent three days praying, fasting, and working on vision, mission, and core values for the church. This is important for every business, but somehow many churches and nonprofits do not emphasize these as much. Again, we put up Post-it notes around the room, and wrote down a lot of ideas and dreams. Then we began the hard work of "wordsmithing" phrases down to where we knew God was glorified, these phrases would set a direction, and people would remember them. There is power in words. You need to pray and find the right words and phrases that people will remember about your ministry. Businesses spend days and countless dollars to craft catchy statements they use inside their business as well as for advertising their products to the world. In fact, I bet you can identify many businesses simply by their slogans.

Strategic planning and wordsmithing are important for churches and nonprofits as well. Coming up with vision and mission statements as well as core values helps keep your church or nonprofit focused on what God has called you to do. If you don't have these defined, then your organization can drift quickly off course. All of these help you stay laser-focused on God's call and help you make a greater impact for God's glory. Out of those three days, we came up with the following:

- The vision statement for Rolling Hills: "A people of God, reaching out, growing up, giving all." This was something we prayed that people could remember and that would keep us tied together and moving forward as God's church.
- The mission statement for Rolling Hills: "Rolling Hills exists to bring glory to God by reaching people for Christ and nurturing them in the faith through inspired worship, genuine community, and passionate ministry that transforms lives in our neighborhoods and throughout the world." This was a little longer, but we wanted it to embody the mission of what God was calling us to do as His church.
- The core values of Rolling Hills: "Love, Reach, Grow, Minister, Joy, Change, Excellence, and Prayer." These would be what would hold us together across all ministries and keep us aligned to God's plans and His purposes.

It is truly amazing how these strategic planning times have impacted us over these first twenty years. We have held on to what God revealed to us in that time and have used it to measure the decisions we make today. Defining who you are and where you are going is essential to who you become.

In addition to strategic planning times for the church, we have also had significant times with our nonprofit, Justice & Mercy International. At one of our first strategic planning sessions, we prayed and crafted the vision, mission, and core values for JMI:

- The vision statement of Justice & Mercy International: "We envision a time when justice has truly been made personal and the gospel has been clearly communicated to and modeled for the people of all the places where God has called JMI and His church to work."
- The mission statement for Justice & Mercy International: "Our mission is to make justice personal for the poor, the orphaned, and the forgotten people of the world."
- Then, since there is so much ministry to do, we decided to make it very clear what we would do as JMI through our core values: "Human Trafficking Prevention, Crisis and Family Care, Pastor Training and Equipping, Vulnerable Child and Teen Care, and Church Mobilization." This helps us to stay focused when there are so many needs and opportunities.

Once you have taken the time to plan, then you have a direction and a filter for the church or nonprofit going forward. Every business has to know what they are supposed to do, and if they take on too much, then they will go down. The same is true in the church and nonprofit world, so being laser-focused is the key. Now, when there are needs or opportunities, we can make sure they align with our vision and mission. Strategic planning times are essential for businesses as well as for churches and nonprofits.

In addition, after the initial planning time, we have an annual three-day strategic planning retreat to make sure we stay aligned. As Andy Stanley says, "vision leaks."[7] After a while, if you don't revisit and assess where you are and where you are going, then you can find yourself off track. Scheduling time to reevaluate the vision and the mission is a must. Everything changes with time. What may have been necessary a few years ago may not be important now. Periodic strategic planning retreats are helpful to focus on the actual objectives of your organization. The world we live in changes quickly. We need to be looking ahead, or we will always find ourselves trying to lead from behind.

> *We need to be looking ahead,*
> *or we will always find ourselves*
> *trying to lead from behind.*

What has also been helpful for us is Strat Ops. This is a business planning strategy that helps the leaders and the organization assess their direction and set a plan for the future. There are times when you need an outside voice—someone outside the organization to help you see what is happening from a different point of view. We have used consultants at different times and people who are actually trained in Strat Ops. Sometimes as a leader you are so close to a situation that you need someone outside to come in and ask the "Why?" questions without a personal attachment. An outside point of view is always helpful. You don't have to implement everything they suggest, but it's good to hear challenges to what we are doing and think about ways we can do ministry better. As I mentioned earlier, as a church staff we find the time of meeting with churches so valuable as we can learn from what others are doing.

Also, as an aside, it is important for each leader to take the time to develop a personal mission statement. I encourage you to pray and ask God what He wants you to do. A personal mission statement can help you focus and eliminate distractions in your life. The fact is: you can't do everything, so you must focus your life. You have a limited amount of time and resources. Therefore, when you plan where to allocate those resources, you can have a greater impact with your life. This works just as well for families in creating a family mission statement.

Identifying Your Unique Contribution

Every leader and every organization has the opportunity to make a unique contribution to the world. God would not have called you or your ministry to start if someone else could do exactly what you do and for exactly the same people. You are gifted, called, and unique. The problem is that many leaders and organizations lose their focus. Whether they end up copying others around them or the busyness of ministry becomes too consuming, they end up moving away from their unique calling. Mission statements and core values help leaders and organizations stay focused. You learn from others, but you must keep the unique calling that defines you and your ministry. The goal is not to always be the greatest, but to always be who God called and created you and your ministry to be.

There are so many needs in the world today. There are a lot of places where we need to engage. However, your church or nonprofit cannot do everything. You need to pray for clarity as to your unique contribution and pray for other churches and nonprofits as they minister. We are all on the same team. While there are a lot of great nonprofits and ministries in the world that work with orphans today, what we as a new church found at the time we started, back in 2003, was that there weren't many working in Moldova. We knew this was a unique contribution that we could make to the kingdom, and these kids needed help. We made the commitment to invest deeply in this country of Moldova. God was calling us to do that. What is God calling you to do?

As a church, we partner with a lot of ministries. We have been on mission trips to South Africa, Ecuador, Haiti, Peru, and many other places around the world. We partner today by sending prayers and money to many different local, national, and international ministries. We are big believers in strategic partnerships. But we also want to be true to the unique calling God has given to us as His church. For us, it was Moldova, and then the unreached people of the Amazon jungle.

Stay focused. We can't do everything, but we can all do something. As you pray, fast, and ask God to make His plans clear to you, He will show you. Stay committed to the strategic plan He gives you. There are so many other places where we could also be, but we have decided to dive deep into these two places in the world. Over the years, we have seen God do miracles there—it is where we believe we can make a unique contribution for God's glory.

Middle Tennessee, Moldova, and the Amazon are our places. We pray and invest deeply in each of these areas. Who knew twenty years ago that Nashville would become such a hot market and people would be moving here from all over? God knew—so He had us plant a church, then have multiple campuses to reach different areas of Middle Tennessee where people are moving. There are other amazing churches in our community, and we pray with them and join with them in making a difference for Christ. Who knew there would be a global pandemic that would impact Brazil especially? God knew, so He had us already serving in the Amazon jungle areas and the Brazilian government asking to partner with us to supply oxygen, masks, sanitation, doctors, and more through our network to the entire Amazonas region. God saved so many lives physically and spiritually in that time. Who knew there would be a war between Russia and Ukraine that was on the border of Moldova? God knew, so He had us already there with forty-five Moldovan staff to meet the needs of Ukrainian refugees coming into Moldova. Trust Him and invest deeply where He calls you. You can make a unique contribution to the kingdom.

Dream

What would you do if money were no object?

Pray, fast, and dream. Think about how churches and believers in the past made such a significant impact in the world for the glory of God. Dream about what God could do through you and your church, nonprofit, and ministry. What if God calls you to share Jesus with every person in your community? If not you, then who? What if God calls you and your church to eradicate poverty in your city? What if God calls you to feed all the hungry or clothe all those needing clothes? What if God calls you to reach every person in your local prison? Dream big.

Few dreams become a reality without stepping out in faith and taking a risk. Every now and then, launch a new program or a new ministry. Be innovative and creative. Businesses do this all the time. They take the time to do the research to know what is effective now. While God does not change, everything else changes. What worked to accomplish the church's mission fifty years ago might not work today. This is a part of life and ministry. There are still churches that think it is the 1980s or '90s—same songs, buildings, pews, etc. It's time to change. Have a "secret shopper" come in and give you insights from a different perspective. We grow used to our "sameness," and while it is comfortable, it is probably not effective (or at least, as effective as it could be). Every year, there needs to be some "spring cleaning" at home and in your organization. Businesses know that if they don't change, then they won't survive. Churches and nonprofits can hang on—especially if they have one big donor. But once something happens to that donor, then it is all over. And we are not here to simply serve a donor, but to serve Jesus. We must constantly be willing to change. Someone once wrote, "You are never too old to set another goal or to dream a new dream."[8]

Work in Your Strengths

Business and finances are not typically strengths for most pastors or nonprofit leaders. Most leaders are in ministry because of a specific call to ministry as well as a deep desire to help others. However, even if business is not an area of strength, it can still be an area in which you can succeed. Enlisting the help of people around you is essential. As a leader, you must constantly be moving into your strengths. In other words, if your strength is teaching, then keep giving away the business, organizational, and administrative sides of the ministry to others who are gifted in these areas. This can be volunteers in the church, staff people you hire, or outside companies or contractors. This will benefit the entire organization. If your strength is people, then delegate your "time drainers" to others so that you can be in your strength—with people.

Look at this passage of Scripture: "And He personally gave some to be apostles, some prophets, some evangelists, some pastors and teachers, for the training of the saints in the work of ministry, to build up the body of Christ, until we all reach unity in the faith and in the knowledge of God's Son, growing into a mature man with a stature measured by Christ's fullness" (Eph. 4:11–13). What this is saying is that you don't have to do everything. Right? God called you to be a spiritual leader, and your job is to empower others to use their gifts to do ministry. There are people in our churches and nonprofits who have various gifts that we don't. Find them and invite them to join the work. Some have business skills, planning skills, or administrative skills that can help you and your ministry, and your job is to enlist them to do so.

Are you empowering others to do the work of ministry? Are you growing disciples who serve? Sometimes we want to do it all, but this is not our job. Our job is developing people. In business, the goal is to turn a profit, and many times, people are a means to this end. However, in ministry, *people* are the end. We value people over money. Our call is to develop people to become fully mature disciples. Make sure your planning centers around leading others to Jesus and growing fully mature disciples.

How do you change the world? One life at a time. Believe it, invest your life in it, and take the time to plan for it. God wants to use you to make a unique contribution for His kingdom. Don't bury your gifts or your talents. Be bold and invest in God's work. God will multiply what He has entrusted to you if you are faithful. And He will impact many lives in the process for His glory. Do the hard work of planning, praying, and preparing. Then watch God's work flourish!

Chapter 10

GROWING THE MINISTRY

When we first planted the church, we were trying to figure out how to let the community know we even existed. We wanted to reach people who were not currently attending a church. Our goal was not simply to swap people from one church to another but to reach the 70 percent of the population in our city that were unchurched people in our area. In order to do this, we needed to go where people are and engage them in their life. Most of the mailers and internet marketing at the time were very expensive, so we knew we had to be creative. I was talking with one of the guys in our little gathering at the clubhouse who said, "Why don't we do a 3-on-3 basketball tournament for the community? Our community is passionate about sports, so let's do something that will connect with men, women, teenagers, and kids." We all thought it was a great idea, but again, we didn't have the money. However, we thought if people paid to play, we could do the work to make the event happen and create awareness about the church and Jesus in our community.

The movie theater in the middle of our community had a big parking lot, with a Chick-fil-A adjacent to it. We went to talk to the owner-operator of the Chick-fil-A to see if he would partner with us in this endeavor. After meeting with us, he said, "This is a great idea! We want to be a part of it. In fact, I will put in $5,000 to the event." That was as much as our monthly budget for the entire first year of the church! We ordered basketball goals, found a DJ and sound system, put up posters in Chick-fil-A, and began spreading the word. We were excited!

Three days before the event, we had one team signed up. One. The guy in our little gathering asked, "Do you think we should cancel?" I responded, "No way. God has brought us this far, and He will accomplish His will." We went back to Chick-fil-A and asked if we could put up a goal in the parking lot and give people a free Chick-fil-A sandwich if they made a free throw. He agreed. We spent the next two days shooting free throws and eating Chick-fil-A sandwiches. When the tournament came, we had over thirty teams and it was a huge success. The next year we had sixty teams, and the following year there were over a hundred teams and over five thousand people watching and taking part in the "Family Fun Day" we created in the parking lot. Pretty soon, everyone knew about Rolling Hills Community Church.

It doesn't matter how great your church or ministry is—if no one knows about it, then they will never come. Jesus told an amazing parable about the sower in Matthew 13:3–8, when a farmer went out to sow his field. Some of the seed fell on the road and the birds came and ate it up. Some of the seed fell on the rocky soil, and it sprang up quickly. But because the soil was shallow, it had no roots, so it died off. Then some of the seed fell among the thorns, and even though it grew, the weeds choked it out. But some of the seed fell on good soil where it yielded a harvest thirty-, sixty-, and even a hundredfold.

The parable is about the Word of God being planted in people's hearts. We all know people who fall into all these categories that Jesus mentioned. Some have hardened hearts to the good news of the gospel, others become excited when they hear about Jesus but have no roots so they fall away, and still others are excited about church or serving but they become busy with life, jobs, kids, and more and stop growing. But there are some who hear about Jesus, and grow and share Him with others.

The law of sowing and reaping especially applies for churches and nonprofits. They say it takes "seven touches" for a consumer to buy a product. The same principle applies in ministry. God can change a heart in a moment, but it may take seven distinct touches for a person to trust you or your ministry. This can be the testimony of a friend, a post on social media, a sign, an ad they hear on the radio, a flyer in the mail. Marketing matters. Effective marketing matters even more because it increases the ministry and allows us to help more people. Never be afraid to tell your story. We'll discuss the importance of developing a comprehensive marketing strategy for your ministry or church. God wants us to tell His story. We can do this right and well, and the results will be incredible.

Overcome the Challenges

It's not easy to grow ministries in today's world. We are living in a post-Christian culture. Not everyone is friendly to the things of God, and there are even people who are antagonistic to God's work. We live in a different time and era. What worked in the past will not always work today or in the future. We must be willing to change, to pray, and to try new approaches to ministry.

When I first felt God's call to plant a church, I met with a denominational church training program. They did a church planting assessment and then put me in a cohort with fifteen other church planters. I remember the statistics that said 80 percent of new churches fail. This was . . . less than encouraging. While I believe this statistic has improved over the last twenty years (and it is definitely better with the multisite approach), this statistic turned out to be true for our cohort. As far as I know, only two of the fifteen churches that were planted back in this cohort are still going today. Thankfully, we are one of them.

How you start matters. The bigger the start, the more momentum you have to carry you along. This means putting a lot of energy into a grand opening, launching a website, investing dollars into Google ads, and more to create a buzz at the beginning. But then you need to staff and plan for growth. Being a well-meaning, godly servant is essential, and God's hand of blessing and favor must stay on you for the ministry to flourish, but the basic business principles in this book can also help you create and sustain long-term ministry growth.

The Importance of Marketing

Marketing is a bad word to a lot of people, especially when applied to the context of ministry. But marketing is simply telling your story and inviting others to join in what God is doing. As a leader of a church or nonprofit, you are the lead storyteller. Your role is to tell the story of your church or ministry to anyone who will listen (and even to those who are at first indifferent). No one can tell the story like you. People want to hear. Our world is longing for "good news." We have the greatest story to tell. People want to hear about life change and the good things that are happening. Whether in blogs, letters, platforms, or staff meetings, your call is to share a story so engaging that people cannot help but want to hear and respond.

You also must figure out ways to tell the story outside of your own ministry. Social media is a great way to do this. Be diligent in your postings. Have a plan and a purpose. Invite others to help you and join you in this. Use Google ads and other ways to share the good news online and invite others into the Greater Story. When we first started, our biggest expenditure was our website. As we covered earlier in chapter 7, we must invest heavily online. We have discovered that almost everyone who comes to the Rolling Hills Franklin campus has watched at least one or two sermons online.

No one knows the story as well as you do. Whether through online, events, mailers, or even going door to door, you need to pray and discern the best way to share God's story in your local context. People are looking for help and hope today. Be bold, be wise, and try new ways to "market" your ministry.

Casting the Vision

Where churches and nonprofits must be better than businesses is in casting vision, sharing with people the "why" behind our view that we should be involved and make a difference. Businesses can meet a short-term need, but in ministry, the impact is eternal. While businesses can go after venture capital money, churches rely on the Spirit of God and on the investment of His people. Our job is to cast a compelling vision to invite people to be involved in God's work. This is both our greatest leadership challenge and greatest opportunity.

> *Our job is to cast a compelling vision to invite people to be involved in God's work.*

Money follows vision. People want to invest in God's work. And when they see the results of what your church or nonprofit is doing for the kingdom of God, then people will want to invest. This is why you cannot simply cast the vision once and then move on to something else. As a leader, you must constantly cast the vision and explain the "why" of what you are doing. People want to be a part of something bigger than themselves.

As a leader, you cast the vision to your volunteers, part-time staff, and full-time staff to the point where they can cast the vision themselves.

As they become more and more passionate, they invite others to join in as well. This is how the work multiplies. Keep casting vision and reaching out. God will grow His work. We always think money is the issue. While money can be a challenge, we must never forget that God holds all the riches of the world in His hands. There is power in prayer. Prayer is inviting God into a situation. Prayer is opening our eyes to see the way God sees. Always be casting vision and praying for God to do what only God can do! Remember, God wants His church and ministry to grow.

Research & Development

One of the craziest things we as a church have done to reach people with the good news of Jesus and serve our community is something we tried fifteen years ago. One day we were preparing for Christmas Sundays and events at church, and we thought, "Where are people who don't know Jesus at Christmas? They may come to church if someone invites them, but if not, then they will most likely be at the mall. Everyone goes to buy Christmas presents at some point." So, we decided to set up a table in the middle of the mall and wrap gifts for free. We talked to the management at the mall and received permission (this is important), and then we started wrapping gifts for free. People couldn't believe it! It caught on like wildfire. People came from all over. We were overwhelmed but so excited that first year.

The next year, we went bigger. And by the third year we had a guy in our church build out a big booth, and we literally had volunteers sign up to wrap gifts for free from Black Friday to Christmas Eve. It was a crazy undertaking, but we have people who love to serve and love to wrap. One year, we wrapped over twenty thousand gifts for free. We had no clue whether it would work, but we wanted to try something to reach and serve our community. I don't know how many more years we will do it since more and more people are shopping online, but it definitely has worked so far. Who knows how that might look in the years to come.

Never be afraid to try something new. In fact, if you are not trying new things to reach people for Christ and to grow disciples, then you will not be relevant in the coming years. The problem for the church and many nonprofits is that we don't like to change. We like things the way they are. But our world is changing, and we need to be on the forefront of kingdom impact and not left behind to die with no significant impact.

We need more followers of Jesus like the apostles. These were the ones who were starting new churches and new ministries. We must be bold and start new works. If this is not you, then there must be some people in your church or nonprofit with this gift. Spend time with them and listen to some of their God-given ideas. Take a flier every once in a while and try something new. You will be glad you did, and others will be impacted.

Companies all over the world invest millions or billions of dollars into research and development. If they don't, they know that they will get behind the times and lose their competitive edge. The world is moving too fast, and change is inevitable. At some point, culture will pass them by and they will become obsolete. The same is true in ministry. If we do not invest time and resources in research and development, then we will be less effective in our ministry. We must stay ahead by investing in new ways to do ministry, new ways to impact people and make a difference in their lives. Not every new idea will work, but we still must be willing to try. We need to allocate money for new initiatives, and then we need to evaluate them well. What works today may not work tomorrow. We need to be entrepreneurial in our calling and our ministry. God's church (worldwide) will never go away, but local churches and specific ministries can fail. Many close their doors every year. We must stay true to God's Word but always be looking for innovative ways to engage people with the love of Christ. In this chapter, we will explore ways to stay culturally relevant yet biblically sound as we endeavor to share the love of Christ in our day and in our generation.

Be open and willing to try new ways to reach your community and expand the work of your church or nonprofit ministry. Over the years, in addition to the 3-on-3 basketball tournaments, we have hosted amazing Daddy-Daughter Balls (some of my favorite memories), Father & Son Bowl football games, Taste of Franklin with local restaurants, Christmas concerts with our own and other musical artists, 5K and 10K races to raise awareness and money for missions, just to name a few. All of these have been great events for the community where everyone has had a wonderful time and incredible goodwill and awareness for our church, missions, kids' ministry, and more.

Build a Great Brand and Protect It

Even when we had fifteen people as a young start-up church, we put a lot of our initial capital into developing great brochures and a great website. Every piece of communication is critical, from an online presence to building signage to business cards. One of the most important people on your team is your graphic designer—whether volunteer, contract, part-time, or full-time, you need someone. This position is sharing with the world what you value. Your brand is important, and protecting the quality of your brand is necessary for what people remember. You are always communicating either excellence or mediocrity. Never forget that details matter.

The brand for your church or nonprofit is important. If you look like you care, then people will respond. Everything communicates—be intentional with what and how you communicate. Test your market. See what people respond to as far as your logo and look. Then, once you find the right thing, stick with it. Use your website, social media, the metaverse, and more to share your brand and your story.

Brand-building is not just the job of a graphic designer or the communications team. It's not just pictures and designs, but also words. It's a tedious thing for many people, but it's important to adhere to a style guide. Think about the Nike swoosh or the Apple logo. They have a distinct look and feel, and now everyone knows them. Develop this for your church or nonprofit. Create a look, feel, and standard. My wife, Lisa, is a graphic designer. She created the logo and look for our church. It's been amazing to see the creation of this look and how it has stayed relevant for twenty years. It helps us to stay relevant, consistent, and clear in all our communications to those inside the congregation and outside in the community. Maybe it is time to develop your brand or do a rebrand.

The Message Stays the Same, but the Methods Change

The message of Jesus' redemptive work for all of us on the cross and His resurrection from the dead has stayed the same for two thousand years. Praise God for His message of hope and life. How we communicate His message today is different from in the time of His first disciples. Different language, culture, images, and examples. The message stays the same, but our methods must constantly change to impact our community and generation for Jesus.

Years ago, churches would buy ads in the yellow pages to reach their community, then it moved to newspapers. Today, it's Google ads and social media. Tomorrow, it will be something else. Every church and nonprofit must analyze the methods that will reach their community. Every organization has a limited amount of dollars, so they must be realistic about what is the best use of those dollars and the most effective strategy for sharing their message. If something is not working, then they shouldn't continue doing it. They must be willing to change the methods in order to be effective.

You can't do everything, so be the best at what God has called you to do. Don't spend all your time comparing yourself to other churches or nonprofits. Learn from everyone around you, but develop your own unique "voice" in ministry. You have a sphere of influence that others will never have. You have a specific calling on your life, so be true to God and be bold in using your gifts, talents, and opportunities for His glory.

Part 6

Passion
Personal Call & Investment

Two essential factors in developing healthy, long-term growth in churches and nonprofits are staying focused on your mission and having great people around you. First, stay focused. There is a tendency for all organizations to drift from their original purposes. You can see this especially by looking at Harvard, Yale, and other Ivy League schools that were started to be Christian universities for higher learning. Somewhere along the way, their mission drifted from growing fully mature disciples in Jesus to pursuing knowledge and making money. You must do everything you can to protect the mission and vision of your ministry so you can faithfully accomplish God's original purpose.

Second, the most important part of all great ministries is the people who serve there. Hiring the right people is more critical than ever. Surrounding yourself with the right team of paid and volunteer staff is essential to the long-term success of your organization. There have been many great leaders who have planted churches and started nonprofits, but the key to greater impact is developing the community of leadership and empowering the next generation to lead the organization to even greater global impact for Christ and His kingdom.

Chapter 11

HEALTHY CULTURE

On the first Monday of every month, we gather with our entire staff team from Rolling Hills and Justice & Mercy International for an all-staff celebration. This is one of my favorite times. It is here that we celebrate birthdays and staff anniversaries. We have breakfast, sometimes play a fun game, and spend time in prayer. It is truly a celebration and keeps us all together and headed in the same direction. We make it fun and exciting, and everyone on staff loves it and looks forward to it. We put a lot of energy into it, and it helps us keep a healthy staff culture.

When we were in our early years, we had a smaller staff team. Even then, we recognized the importance of developing a healthy community. A friend of mine told me about the Disney Institute in Orlando. One morning, I asked our team to come in early because we had a surprise event for the day. When everyone showed up for work, I told them we were going on a field trip. We had some friends at church who had frequent flier miles on Southwest Airlines, so we took an early morning flight down to Orlando and were booked to return that same evening.

We arrived that morning at the Disney Institute. Not all the things that Disney does are worth emulating, but there are some definite principles that are transferable to church and nonprofit leadership. When we arrived, we had a wonderful guide who took us on a tour. We started underground at Disney where the "cast" (what Disney calls their employees) spends their time preparing the "magic" that happens. Our guide talked about how much time Disney spends recruiting and training cast members. This was their number one priority. These are the people, she said, "that make the magic happen."

Someone on our team asked what they do if a "cast" member does not fit the Disney culture. She graciously said, "We help them find their happiness elsewhere." The way she said it was not negative, but more along the lines of the importance of finding the right fit for their culture. She even emphasized this point by saying that they listen to how cast members tell the story of Disney. They help them learn to use the word "we" instead of "them." Even though they were not there in the early days, they tell the story with passion and ownership because they are part of the bigger story now. It is their story too. Then, they know they are in the Disney culture. They are passionate about developing the right community.

In business and ministry, we must develop people who are passionate about the organization. Building passionate followers does two things: (1) it creates momentum in the number of people who can be helped, and (2) it sets the organization up to win in the future. Too many times, a ministry or a church is dependent on one leader or on one significant donor. But what happens when that leader or donor leaves or dies? The ministry often falls apart. Developing a community of leadership and passionate investors is essential for the long-term sustainability of the ministry. In a church, Jesus called us to "make disciples" (Matt. 28:19). We must be pointing people constantly to Jesus. As people fall in love with Jesus, their lives will be transformed. Creating a culture where people love Jesus and are passionate about serving is essential for your church or ministry. We will look at how we can develop followers who love Jesus first and foremost, and then are passionate about living out His calling in your church or ministry.

Developing a community of leadership
and passionate investors is essential
for the long-term sustainability
of the ministry.

Make it your goal to have a healthy culture in the church or nonprofit where you serve. As Jesus said, "By this all people will know that you are My disciples, if you have love for one another" (John 13:35). Your ministry should be defined by love, and this starts with your leadership team and then flows to your staff and those you serve. What kind of culture do you have in your organization? Is it healthy or not? If not, then pray and work to develop the right community.

Find the Right People

Whether hiring full-time staff or recruiting volunteers, having the right people on your team is essential. Take your time in hiring for a new staff position. First, it is a big expense to bring on a full-time person, so make sure you bring on the right people. It takes time to interview, vet, check references, and potentially relocate someone and their family. Be sure to interview a lot of people for the position (and even use a reputable search firm if needed). Pray fervently for this person to be the right fit. Then, always do a ninety-day evaluation to make sure they are on the right track with the ministry as a whole and that they feel good about being in the position and on the team. You can learn so much from new employees because they see the ministry with fresh eyes.

When there are challenges—and there will be, because none of us are perfect—address the challenges or concerns that person has. People matter. And joyful, fulfilled, satisfied people are what build your culture. If there is a problem, don't take years to address it. Do a PIP (performance improvement plan) if you need to, to give better direction to that person. This will help everyone stay headed in the right direction. If there is not a good fit with an employee, then work with them to find a solution in the organization or help them make a needed change. Sometimes things don't work out, and that's hard. We have had very few of these times at Rolling Hills or JMI over the years (thank You, God), but there are times when, as a leader, you have to be willing to make a hard decision and help them "find their happiness somewhere else."

You always want to keep the relationship and to take care of the person as best you can. Everyone has a calling and a family. People want to do their best. The win is when it works out for everyone. Always err on the side of grace and love. Do the right thing in severance and go over and above industry standards to take care of someone. But overall, you can't keep the wrong people in an organization if they are bringing down the culture. You need to be the leader and make the best decisions for the organization as well as for every person on your team.

The 3 Cs

There are 3 Cs when it comes to hiring new staff, recruiting volunteers, or monitoring how someone fits into your culture. The first C is Character. You can never compromise on this one. I don't care how great a candidate looks online. I don't care if they are a rock star in their field. In ministry, you can never compromise on character. Character is who you are when no one is watching. In ministry, we must be above reproach. Character and integrity are first and foremost to developing a healthy, godly community.

Integrity with money, appropriate interactions with staff and others, trust—these are all areas where you cannot compromise. One bad hire can impact the entire organization. If you have a "check in your spirit" when you are interviewing someone, or you keep hearing some questionable reports about a volunteer, step in and act. Move that person along and help them "find their happiness elsewhere."

Now, people will make mistakes. We all do. And as leaders, our job is to help people correct those mistakes and help them become the best version of themselves. This is part of discipleship; sanctification. However, it's important to consider when someone does make a mistake whether they are remorseful and willing to learn. Are they teachable and coachable? Are they seeing where they can improve? Do they understand why doing the right thing matters?

Many times in business, questionable decisions are tolerated or even appreciated if they lead to additional revenue for the corporation. But in business there is a crackdown on ethical code of conduct violations and even government regulations that monitor character decisions. But, as Christian organizations, our standard should be even higher than that. We must never compromise on character. Care enough to confront poor behavior in the staff, the volunteers, or the organization itself. Church discipline has gone by the wayside in many congregations today, but it is important for developing a healthy, godly community. Be willing to have the hard conversations and surround yourself with people who will do what is right for themselves, the ministry, and their Savior.

The second C is Competency. You need to develop a high-performance team. You need a place where people know what they are doing and do it well. When you are hiring or looking for the right people to volunteer, being sure that people know what they are doing is important. You can teach and you can train, but bringing someone in who has a high competency for the position will help everyone.

In business, people develop their competencies through education— undergraduate studies and graduate school along with internships—and previous work experiences. In church and nonprofit work, there are not as many undergraduate degrees, and seminary is great for theological development but not always the best for practical ministry competency. Again, there are internships and continuing education seminars and programs available, but these are not as widespread as business opportunities. We must always push ourselves to grow in our competency. We can learn from other churches and nonprofits and do our own research, and then empower our team as well.

Finding people who are good at what they do and are willing to take the initiative to develop themselves is important and essential for growing your organization. There is so much content available today. There are online classes, books, blogs, and other resources to help people grow in their serving and leading capacities. As a leader, you must help your team grow in their work competency. Hire as best you can. Hire people who will challenge you to be better. Pray for and surround yourself with people who have a high competency.

The third C is Chemistry. This is big as well. You need to find the right people who are a good fit for your team. As the business guru Peter Drucker allegedly said, "Culture eats strategy for breakfast." It doesn't matter how great your plans and dreams are if you don't have the right people around you to accomplish your God-given vision.

Just look at sports teams. You can have teams with great talent. But if they don't get along and there is trouble in the clubhouse or locker room, then that team will implode. Chemistry, along with call and vision, is what makes people want to come to work, to church, or to your ministry. People want to feel valued and appreciated. Creating a great culture begins with hiring people who are a great fit.

Even with volunteers, if someone is negative all the time, it will bring the entire organization down over time. Lead with people who believe in what you are doing and who want the best for your organization. Remember, we have an enemy who wants to destroy the culture and community. Pray for God's protection over your church and nonprofit. The devil would love to get a foothold in your ministry, and many times he does that through one or two people on your team. Pray, lead, and elevate culture. Surround yourself with people who are high in all three Cs and watch your church or nonprofit flourish.

The Importance of Accountability

In every business, there is a board of directors to help give oversight to the company. The business is not built on one person, but as a corporation. Every ministry needs accountability. When we planted Rolling Hills, I knew the church should not be about me. Since we incorporated as a 501(c)(3) for tax-exempt status, we are required, like every church and nonprofit, to have a board of directors. In some churches, the board of trustees is made up of elders or deacons. However you decide who should be part of this leadership team, it's important that you have this in place and use it well. Accountability and support for the staff, leaders, and members of the organization is essential to long-term success.

In any ministry area, it is important to think about having a personal board of directors. It is so beneficial to have wise, godly people around you. We all need accountability and support in our own lives. Ministry is not easy. Too many times, those in ministry go through hard seasons of having no one to walk with them. As ministry leaders, we need wise counsel around us. There are tough decisions to make. In addition, ministry leaders face burnout, mental health struggles, and other significant challenges. This is why we need a ministry board and a personal board to walk with us through the hard times and celebrate with us in the good times.

The breadth of your ministry is contingent on the depth of your community. Those who try to go alone do not go far. An old African proverb says, "If you want to run fast, run alone. If you want to run far, run together." We need others. This is true for all ministries. Don't go alone—ministry can be lonely enough. You are unable to carry all your problems, as well as the problems of all those in your congregation or ministry area. We need others to carry the burden with us. Even Jesus surrounded Himself with twelve others. Jesus didn't need them to hold

Him accountable, but we do need that. Although we are striving to be like Jesus (Rom. 8:29), none of us are there, so we need others walking this journey with us.

Retaining Key Leadership

Successful ministries and organizations have longevity in their key positions—both volunteers and staff. As the old saying goes, "Hire slowly, and fire quickly." Hopefully, you don't have to fire too often. This will come down to how you hire on the front end. It takes time to find the right people. Once you have great people, take care of them. Flexible work schedules and time off are important. Insurance and benefits are becoming as important as base salary. And there are other ways to help keep and strengthen great leaders.

There is a difference between how you handle employees in ministry versus business. Yes, there are still employment laws, but there is a difference between those laws for publicly traded companies and for privately owned ones. As churches and nonprofits, there is protection for hiring people who are Christ followers and for moving people along who do not align with the vision and mission of the organization. However, as ministries, we should be held to a higher standard in how we treat people. We should always err on the side of grace. Tough decisions must be made when it comes to budget constraints or cuts, but always take care of your people and this will translate into the long-term health of your organization.

Ministries and businesses also differ in how we measure results—churches and nonprofits are not based on shareholders' approval, but on growing disciples of Jesus and ministering to others. Therefore, you need key leadership to be in place long-term to develop relationships and discipleship. This may mean slower growth, but remember that there is a greater long-term result in light of eternity. We're not talking about a daily stock price as the measure, but about surrounding yourself with people who are committed to the organization for the long haul.

In order to do this well, you need to invest in your people. As they grow deeper in their personal walk with the Lord, as they grow stronger in their leadership capacity, and as they grow further in their influence and impact, your entire ministry organization grows as well. At Rolling Hills, we are constantly looking for feedback from our staff. We do take the "Best Places to Work" survey or the "Best Christian Workplaces" survey every year. By God's grace, we have always scored exceptionally well. Having an outside measure helps to evaluate any staff culture. If you have high turnover with your staff, then take the time and energy to fix it. Having the right staff team and the right culture is essential to church health.

I am so blessed because we have an incredible staff team at both Rolling Hills and Justice & Mercy International. Our team loves God and truly loves each other. We have been together a long time, and as leadership, we are always trying to bless, encourage, and empower one another as well as the amazing people our God has entrusted to our care. As our staff team grows personally and spiritually, the entire church and nonprofit grows as well. I love our team, and I am so thankful to serve our great God with each and every one. Your staff team sets the pace for the church or nonprofit. Nurture and take care of your staff.

Businesses are known to do a much better job than churches and nonprofits at helping to develop their staff. In business, there are ninety-day reviews, performance reviews, mid-year and annual reviews. Businesses know the importance of giving feedback and helping grow their people. In our churches and nonprofits, we can all become better at this. People want to know where they stand. People want to know if they are doing a good job or not. Yet, often churches or nonprofits are not willing to speak the truth because they don't want to hurt someone's feelings. But how can anyone become better if they don't receive feedback?

In churches and nonprofits, I encourage you to implement performance reviews for your staff and volunteers. If it helps, change the name from "performance reviews" to "coaching sessions." This is what you are doing—coaching. People want to grow and get better at what they are called to do. When you sit down to a "coaching session," everyone benefits—the staff team member, the volunteer, the leader, and the overall ministry. Let's build, coach, and grow up the best team possible for the glory of our great God.

Chapter 12

DEVELOP THE NEXT GENERATION OF LEADERS

For any ministry or organization to grow, or even sustain long-term, you must constantly be raising up new leaders and growing faithful followers. Sports are big businesses in the United States, whether it be Major League Baseball with their farm system, the National Basketball Association with their D-League ("D" for developmental), or the National Football League with college football and practice squads, there is always a pipeline for developing new talent.

When we started the church, we did not have enough money to pay full-time staff. Our solution was to rent two apartments (one for women and one for men) and have "interns." These would be juniors or seniors in college who felt called to ministry. They would work for rent and, in the process, be our "staff." It was amazing! These young leaders were invaluable. Today, we continue to use the intern program to train future leaders for both our church as well as other churches. Whether volunteers, junior staff, or interns, every ministry must be looking for ways to multiply leadership. Today, we have a robust program called the Leadership Institute, which develops young leaders for future ministry.

Through the Leadership Institute, we have gained full-time ministry employees at all our campuses. In addition, we have seen graduates of the Leadership Institute go on to serve in other churches and nonprofit organizations throughout the country. This is one of the parts of ministry that I am most proud of and most excited about. We have an incredible group of interns and residents, and it makes me encouraged about the future of ministry not only at Rolling Hills and Justice & Mercy International, but in the kingdom overall. I believe millennials and members of Gen Z are more open to the gospel than ever before, and they are ready and willing to make a significant difference with their lives. They have seen the challenges our nation and world are facing, and they want to be a part of the solution. We must find ways to engage them and empower them to make a difference.

Think about how much time and money businesses spend on recruiting talent. Businesses have entire recruiting departments because they know how important this is. Universities spend millions of dollars and employ many people in order to recruit the best students to their schools. Football coaches have huge recruiting departments, and they also get personally involved in recruiting. Nick Saban at the University of Alabama is probably sitting in the home of a seventeen-year-old kid today because he knows this player can win him a national championship in four years. The United States military spends spend an unbelievable amount of time and money on recruiting. And then there is the church and ministries. We, for the most part, do nothing. We are reactionary. When we have a need, we post, hope, and pray for God to bring someone to fill a spot. Instead, we need to be proactive in preparing and raising up the next generation of spiritual leaders. This is exactly what Jesus did. Jesus went out and recruited twelve men who would ultimately lead His church.

Developing Passionate Followers

Growing followers who invest their time, energy, and resources is critical for long-term success. Community looks different today than it ever has. Through social media, developing an online following will help grow your ministry's influence and effectiveness. Every ministry and organization has the opportunity to impact the world. This was not true years ago, but it is today. Creating a community is not just about staff and your local constituency, but now your impact can extend into the entire world. The power of these passionate followers is tremendous.

In business, it is easy to turn off your job. You can clock in and clock out. You show up for your job and do your work because it is transactional—you do this task, and you get paid. There is no relational equity that you must invest. You are there to do a job, and the company is there to pay you for your work.

Ministry is obviously much different. Ministry is highly relational, because Jesus is highly relational. While there is a transactional element—you do your job and receive a wage from the church or nonprofit—most of ministry is more in the relational area of life. You are sharing the love of Jesus with others. You are teaching, counseling, ministering, serving, praying, and investing in others for the glory of God. So much of ministry in the church and nonprofit world is more about your life, investment, and love. Jesus said, "By this all people will know that you are My disciples, if you have love for one another" (John 13:35). How you love becomes the measure. You become the ministry. The way you love, serve, and lead makes such a difference to the church and nonprofit, and ultimately to the kingdom of God.

The Bible tells us that "the worker is worthy of his wages" (1 Tim. 5:18). You should not feel guilty about making money for your work in the church or in a nonprofit. Ministry organizations should always be doing more to take care of their people when it comes to salaries and benefits. A ministry worker should receive a fair wage for their good work. However, in ministry, money should never be our primary motivator. Yes—we need money to help support our life and our family, but ultimately God is our Provider.

When God called us to plant Rolling Hills, I remember someone saying to me, "I know you are thinking about planting a church, but how are you going to support a family?" Actually, through the beginning part of this process, I had never worried about money—until then. When they said this, I immediately started thinking, "Oh no. I can't do this." I had a good job at the time with a good salary and benefits, and church planting meant no salary or benefits for a while. Yet it came down to trusting God to provide. And He did. It meant less money, but God took care of us in those early years while the church was growing. God used His people, and He showed up and showed off. It really became a matter for me to learn to trust in God more than money.

Churches and nonprofit organizations have a responsibility to take care of our people, to pay fair wages and provide benefits for families. As leaders in churches and nonprofits, we should endeavor to be competitive with those in our industry. We need to do it for good morale and to retain talent, but even more because it is the right thing to do. Your people are the ministry. If they are unhappy or disgruntled all the time over not feeling cared for by the leaders in the ministry, then this will come through to everyone around. As ministries, we cannot compete on the same salary scale as businesses, but we must be in line with what it takes to sustain a family in our market.

Sometimes this means that those who serve in ministry need to be bivocational, to have another job outside of ministry in order to make up needed revenue. Remember, the apostle Paul was a tentmaker. He would make tents and then use the money he received to go on mission trips and plant churches. This is very effective in ministry. Also, in today's world, it works to have a side job online: speaking, writing, promoting books or items you or your coworkers create online. There are many ways to earn additional income and help offset the money needed to do the ministry.

Don't Say No for People

Several years ago, when Justice & Mercy International was starting to grow, we had this amazing opportunity to expand the work of ministry into the Amazon region. I remember praying, "Lord, we need a strong leader. We need someone who will take this, lead it, and grow the ministry. The calling and the work are big. Please provide the right person." The person God brought to my mind was a highly successful businesswoman in our church. She had a big job with a lot of responsibility. I knew she was the right one, but I thought there was no way she would take it. I almost didn't even talk to her about it.

But finally, after praying a lot about it, I met with her. She had been a family friend of ours for years, and was one of the first people at Rolling Hills. We could offer her literally half of her salary to take this position. But by God's grace, she took the job. She said, "I don't know what is more miraculous: that I took it or that you offered it to me." People want to be involved in God's work. Today, she is doing an incredible job, and our God has used her leadership to grow the ministry and to impact thousands of orphaned children, river people, and jungle pastors for His glory. She is definitely the right leader, and I almost said no for her.

Pray about the people you need in your church and ministry. Be bold and ask God to bring the right ones to join the work. Don't say no for people. People want to use their gifts not just in business to make money, but to serve the Lord God Almighty. It is the highest calling there is, so pray for God to bring the right people to your church and ministry.

Stick to It

We live in a time where we want immediate results. But it takes time to build anything significant. Many people quit in ministry before they ever see the harvest. In business, as in ministry, a strong work ethic is essential for success. Sometimes churches and nonprofits do not perform to their maximum capacity because the leadership does not work as much as needed. Learning to balance the "seasons" of ministry is important. Some times are busier than others. The churches and nonprofits (and businesses, for that matter) that have made the greatest impact have had leaders as well as leadership teams that have stayed together for the long haul. No church or ministry is perfect. Find the place God has called you, and then invest your life there.

You Can't Do It All

Most people try to do it all, and this is where burnout occurs. As the ministry grows, your leadership must change at each stage of growth. You must always be moving into your area of strength, and you must prioritize your time. As a funeral director told me, "Death knows no weekends or holidays." Everything stops in a crisis—death, marriage problems, trouble with kids—but all the demands of your everyday job and life continue. You have to be willing to say no to some things in order to be able to be present for the things only you can do. You can't do it all. Once you realize this, and stop trying, balance begins to happen in your life.

> *You have to be willing to say no to some things in order to be able to be present for the things only you can do.*

Rest

When you are starting or launching any ministry or business, there is a lot of work to do. After we had been going as a church for a few years, I went off to study one afternoon. It had been an extremely busy season of ministry, so I pulled out my computer and commentaries to work on sermon prep for Sunday. Well, I happened to put my head down for a moment because I was so tired. Then, I remember waking up *three hours later*. I couldn't believe it, but I obviously needed it. My work/life balance was way off, and I needed to rediscover a healthy rhythm in order to go forward.

When God created the world, He introduced rest as well (Gen. 2:2). We all need a day of rest. In ministry, we need to work hard, but we also need to have a healthy work/life balance. People are watching your life to see if you are healthy—spiritually, physically, mentally, socially, and emotionally. This is so important.

Nobody wins when a leader burns out. Where's the balance for those involved in ministry? How do we find time to do ministry, raise a godly family, and experience the abundant life that God desires for us? When we first planted, I knew it would take the favor of God and a lot of hard work for us to succeed. Being on the front lines of ministry is not always easy. Just read through the book of Acts and see all the challenges the apostles endured for the sake of the gospel.

A church or a ministry is like a garden. God gives the soil and the rain for it to grow, but it takes a lot of work from the farmer to make the ground ready and to tend to the harvest. Many times, people are not ready for the hard work it takes to grow a ministry or a church. However, there must be balance on both sides. There is always one more hospital visit to make, one more email needing a response, one more donor to write. Ministry never stops. We all want to succeed at our ministry calling, but we all want our families (or future families) to thrive in the process. There is a way to do both well.

Balancing work and life is beneficial and essential. There are people who live to work and others who work to live. Regardless of your wiring and drive, both are important. God created work before the fall, and He wants you to do your best. But always remember, family first. If you are not healthy at home, then you will not be able to do your best at work. "Balance" is a little bit of a misnomer. There are definitely seasons where things may feel out of balance. In ministry, Christmas and Easter are two of those "busy" seasons. But find a rhythm where you have busier seasons and then you rebalance for health and longevity.

It really comes down to priorities. Our priority must always be to put God above everything. Jesus said, "Seek first the kingdom of God and His righteousness, and all these things will be provided for you" (Matt. 6:33). After God, if you are married, comes your spouse. This is so important. Before your kids or your work is your spouse. You want to have a great marriage, and this takes work and intentionality. After your spouse come your kids, and then comes work. The problem comes when we misalign our priorities. When we put our work over God or our spouse. Or we put our kids over God or our spouse. If we keep the right priorities, then this will help to bring balance into our hearts and lives.

Sometimes the most beneficial thing you can do is to take a nap. If you are worn out all the time, you will eventually not make great decisions. Understanding your "rhythm" in work is important. Sometimes rest can manifest in simply doing some things you enjoy, whether it's spending time with family, vacation, or working out. There needs to be something to give your mind and body rest. Work hard, but work smart. You were built for the long run, so figure out how to incorporate rest in order to sustain the pace and the impact.

Sabbath

One of the Ten Commandments is "Remember the Sabbath day, to keep it holy" (Ex. 20:8). Taking a day off for worship and rest is right up there with "Do not kill" and "Do not steal." Rest is clearly important to God!

In church work especially, it is hard to have a day off. Sundays, everyone else's Sabbath, is the biggest day in ministry. Therefore, you must find a different day to take off for a day of rest. This can be as the original Shabbat—Friday evening through Saturday evening. Or take Mondays or Fridays off to recover. Whatever day it is, it is important to find a day of worship and rest. Not only is it important, it's a commandment. God knows we all need it.

In addition to Sabbath, something else that is important is sabbaticals. God established in the Old Testament that every seven years the land should rest (Ex. 23:11). Therefore, every seven years we allow our staff team to have a one-month sabbatical to rest and recharge. People can use this time to study other ministries, to travel, to be with family and friends, and to recharge their spiritual batteries. This is important for everyone.

Vacation

Every ministry leader needs time to rest as well as time to be with family. Overworking is not a badge of honor. Schedule time away and then take it. When you think about it, someone else can do your job, but no one else can be mom or dad to your kids. We will miss our ultimate calling, the calling to our families, if we allow the demands of business and ministry to rule our lives. There must be a balance.

I want to encourage you to take your vacation. Go be with your family. Make memories. Children grow up quickly. Time flies, and ministry can dominate your life. There is always one more person to visit, card to write, text to send, and yet your family needs you just as much—actually, even more. Go on trips. Get away. The vacation doesn't have to be expensive. Go to a state park and hike. Go visit family or friends who live in a cool city. Find a place and go explore. You need to clear your head, and you need time with your family. It takes planning and time, but it is so worth it.

This is essential for making the greatest impact. This is my prayer for you. Your goal is to stay healthy and faithful all the days the Lord has you on this earth. Then, when God calls you home, to go home victoriously knowing that you gave your all for Christ and His call.

Part 7

Power

God's Work for God's Glory

When you are in ministry, you are doing God's work. And if God is on your side, then you will win. Nothing or no one is greater than Him! Our God works through ministries as well as through followers of Christ in business—and through some amazing businesses themselves. Always remember, where God is, there is power. No matter what we face in life, in business or in ministry, always know our God is greater! He can and does work miracles to fulfill His purposes.

Chapter 13

MIRACLES STILL HAPPEN

Through the years, we have seen miracles at Rolling Hills and JMI. I mean straight-up miracles. This is what I love so much about being on this journey with God. Some people believe that miracles stopped after the first disciples and the establishment of the early church. But I am here to tell you that is not right. Our God still does miracles today. He can, and will, do miracles in your life and in your ministry. As you plan, prepare, and invest your life in building His kingdom, don't forget that you serve a God who is greater. Pray and be bold.

Our God is a Healer. Recently, our pastor of business administration had a massive heart attack. Jim had been on our staff for eight years. Before this, he'd been the CFO of a $100 million a year company in Chicago. Yet, Jim had always had a passion for the Lord and for serving Him with his life. Jim took a pay cut and moved from Chicago to Nashville to be on our church staff. Jim is incredible, and he has brought so much wisdom and business prowess to our church. After dinner one night, Jim was playing hockey in a league. During the game, he had a massive heart attack and fell to the ice. By God's grace, the goalie on the other team was a firefighter. He skated over to Jim and began doing CPR. The rink had an AED machine, and they used it on Jim.

When Jim arrived at Vanderbilt University Medical Center, the situation was dire. They put him in an induced coma to try to stabilize his body. When I arrived to see him, Jim was hooked up to every machine available. He was in the critical care unit. The nurse who was in there did not give him much hope. In fact, one of the doctors said Jim had about a 6 percent chance to live. But Jim, and our church family, has a really big God.

As God's people prayed, He did a miracle. While I am so thankful for doctors, nurses, and modern-day medicine, our ultimate faith is in the Lord God Almighty. He is our Healer. Today, Jim is walking around and feeling great. He is even contemplating hockey again—which his wife is not very keen on! But overall, Jim is a walking, talking testimony to the healing power of God.

God loves your people even more than you do, and He is drawing people to Himself and transforming lives for His glory. He is the One who is redeeming and restoring. He is the One who is loving people through you. He is the One who longs to have a personal relationship with every person you know and serve. Keep praying and sharing God's love boldly. Keep trusting that God can and will do miracles.

God Is Our Provider

God is also our Provider. One of God's names is Jehovah Jireh. *Jireh* means "provider." Jesus taught His followers to call God "Father," and the role of a father is to provide and protect. God promises to provide for you, personally. God loves you, and He loves your ministry. In fact, He loves it more than you do. The church is the "body and bride" of His Son (Eph. 5:25–30). Therefore, God is passionate about your ministry. He may not do what we want Him to do in our timing, but He is the One who is always working—growing and building His kingdom. Even when it seems like you are stuck, never forget that we serve a miracle-working God.

I remember when we bought the warehouse in Franklin. There was some vacant land next door, and we thought if we could buy five acres of land for future parking, then that would be amazing. The land wasn't for sale, but we kept praying. Then, one day, the land went into foreclosure. A guy in our church who is a real estate agent found out about it and let us know. We were able to buy not only five acres but the entire twenty-seven acres. This was truly a miracle. We have been able to expand and grow God's church and His work.

You are a part of God's plan. You are leading and serving in God's ministry. He calls us, and we serve Him. We must always remember that He is sovereign over all. He has called us to steward His work, but He is the One who will make it grow. So many times, we feel the weight of trying to make everything happen. Yet, at the end of the day, we are called to work hard but must always remember it is the power of God that transforms lives. Jesus said, "On this rock I will build My church, and the forces of Hades will not overpower it" (Matt. 16:18).

> *God has called us to steward His work,*
> *but He is the One who will make it grow.*

Because God is sovereign, He can redeem every situation. Whatever you face in your ministry, always remember that God is greater. Often when we are out of ideas, this is where God does His best work. This way, only God receives the glory.

The Power of Prayer

Our last-ditch effort often involves prayer, but prayer should always be our first response and our priority. So many times, we are too busy to pray. But prayer is where the power lies. As Oswald Chambers said, "Prayer does not equip us for greater works—prayer is the greater work."[9] We must learn to pray strategically for God to do miracles in our church and ministry.

What are you praying for God to do that only God can do? Prayer invites God into your ministry. His power is greater than anything we can do. God has all the resources in the world. Through prayer, we invite the God of the universe to work miracles.

Give God the Glory

When God first called us to plant Rolling Hills, I was nervous. All the questions ran in my mind. "God, are You sure? What if this doesn't work?" I remember Lisa calmly saying, "I don't want to look back twenty years from now and think, 'What could God have done if we had only trusted Him and stepped out in faith?' I want to look back twenty years from now and say, 'Look what God did!'" As I write this, we just celebrated our twentieth anniversary, and—wow—look what God has done!

When we started, we had no building, no money, and no staff. But we had a really big God. And that same God is still with us today.

God is building His church. From leasing that first apartment clubhouse to now having multiple campuses, an incredible staff team, the Rolling Hills Learning Center, to the ministry work of Justice & Mercy International, our God is truly at work. We are seeing in a small way how "every day the Lord added to them those who were being saved" (Acts 2:47).

Our theme verse as a church has always been Ephesians 3:20–21: "Now to Him who is able to do above and beyond all that we ask or think according to the power that works in us—to Him be glory in the church and in Christ Jesus to all generations, forever and ever. Amen."

Think about what God is saying to you through this verse. First, *"Now to Him who is able."* Wherever you are and whatever you are facing today—our God is able. He is able to bless you, grow you, and use you in a mighty way for His glory. He is able to overcome the obstacles and win the battles. And He is able *"to do above and beyond all that we ask or think."* God's plans are bigger than your plans. God's dreams for your life, your church, or your ministry are bigger than your own. Wherever you are in ministry, either just starting out or serving for a long time in church or nonprofit work, always invite God to do immeasurably more than you can ask or imagine. He is the One who can do it.

And remember it is *"according to the power that works in us."* It is not your power, but His! The power that raised Jesus from the dead is the same power that is alive in you. Pray bold prayers and step out in faith. Never grow comfortable or complacent. The power of God is in you and working through you. Then, I love *"to Him be glory in the church."* It is God's church or ministry, not your church or ministry. It is God's and God's alone. So give Him the glory He deserves. Amazing things happen when we give all the glory back to God. It is not about us but all about Him. *"And in Christ Jesus to all generations, forever and ever. Amen."* We are a link in the chain. We are called to be faithful in our day and generation so that we can impact the next generation for Christ. Let's work, pray, love, and serve so that the next generation will grow up with a spiritual foundation in Christ and impact their world for Him.

The ministry or the church is not ours but His. When you are faithful to God's calling, God will surprise you. Many times, God's blessings do not come in our timing, but they always come in His timing. There are times when you pray like crazy, and God allows you to go right up to the edge. These are the times when our faith grows and miracles happen. God loves the people your ministry is trying to help even more than you do. We should always hold on to ministry loosely and hold on to God tightly.

We should work hard but always allow God to receive all the glory. If we do this, then people fall in love with God and not with us. Our ministry will not last forever—there is a season for everything—but God is eternal. As people fall in love with Him, then they find help for eternity.

Chapter 14

THE IMPORTANCE OF LEADERSHIP

Today, in most cities and communities, everyone is waiting on politicians to "fix" everything. Homelessness, crime, the need for affordable housing, education, and so much more. Yet, when has the government ever been able to fix everything? It cannot be only about politics. As Christ followers, we should vote. As John Maxwell so famously says, "Everything rises and falls on leadership."[10] You can see the impact of good leaders and bad leaders in nations throughout the world, cities, schools, communities, and churches. However, the government alone cannot fix all the problems. Otherwise, they would have done it by now.

The church and faith-based organizations are essential. Again, we need strong, godly leaders in these organizations. We need you. God has uniquely called you and created you to be a leader. You don't have to do ministry alone. God is with you, and there are other brothers and sisters in Christ who want to lock arms with you to make a difference. What if we join with other godly leaders who are already serving in business, government, schools, or other churches? Then, I believe, together we can truly make a difference.

Colossians 1:28–29 says, "We proclaim Him, warning and teaching everyone with all wisdom, so that we may present everyone mature in Christ. I labor for this, striving with His strength that works powerfully in me." It is not our strength but His strength that works powerfully in us. The same Spirit that raised Jesus from the dead is alive in You! Our job, then, is to grow in the Spirit—to pray, read God's Word, seek wise counsel, and lead out of the Spirit He has placed inside us.

Focus

It's easy for our schedules to become dictated by others. A lot of people in ministry have an overpowering desire to please others. We must always remember the reason why we do what we do. We are called to help people, but God is the One we aim to please. When we release our desire for accolades and attention, then we can truly serve with a pure heart. This allows God to receive the glory and not us.

Don't get distracted with social media, criticism, or the things of this world. It is not about money or success. It is simply about you being focused on Jesus and His call in your life. Live each day and every moment for Him.

Remember Solomon? The wisest and wealthiest man at one point in history? What happened to Solomon is a cautionary tale for all of us. Solomon drifted from God. He fell in love with money and success, and he forgot about God. It was no longer about serving others but about serving himself. This can happen to any of us if we are not careful. Remember the purpose of ministry and the specific call God has given to you. Don't sacrifice your time with the Lord on the altar of worldly success. Don't say, "I'm too busy to pray or to read God's Word or to be around other godly leaders." Your call is to be obedient to God all the days of your life.

Humility

In ministry, it is easy for the work to become about us. Many people have their entire self-esteem and self-worth wrapped up in their performance. When the church or ministry is growing, then people feel good about themselves. When there are challenges or struggles, then it is easy to feel like a failure. We must remember that God receives the glory. Humility means that it is not about us. This way, whether we experience success or struggles, we know that if we are giving our best, God will be glorified. Service is so different from the way the world measures success. In the world, it is about the bigger office, car, or paycheck because it is self-centered. Ministry is about serving, helping, growing, and making a difference in others because it is Christ-centered. The greatest leaders in churches, business, education, and politics are those who are humble and take the focus off themselves.

> *The greatest leaders in churches, business, education, and politics are those who are humble and take the focus off themselves.*

Charles Spurgeon once wrote, "Thus there will be three effects of nearness to Jesus . . . humility, happiness, and holiness."[11] This should be true for every ministry leader. If you are not growing in these areas, then ask yourself, are you moving away from Jesus? As Rick Warren writes, "Humility is not thinking less of yourself; it is thinking of yourself less."[12] Humility is, like Jesus, putting others before yourself. The greatest leaders in business and ministry are the ones who put the needs of others before their own.

Faithfulness

The goal of your life and my life is to hear our God say, "Well done, good and faithful" servant (Matt. 25:21). It is Jesus we are ultimately serving and working for. We can't be good on our own, and this is why we so desperately need Jesus. Once we are in Christ Jesus, then we are good because of the price He paid for us. It is called substitutionary atonement. Jesus took our place, and He paid our price. While we can't be good on our own, we can be faithful, and this is the call for each of us. This is where you see God make the biggest difference—I believe too many people quit in ministry before they truly see God break through. Stay steadfast in the Lord. Stay committed to the call He has on your life. Stay focused, humble, and faithful in your commitment to God and in your ministry to Him.

God Is For You!

God wants your ministry to grow. Things that are alive grow. If you are not growing, even in a small way, then you must ask yourself and your organization some tough questions. You are either growing or declining—there is no middle ground. But the good news is that God can do miracles. If God can raise the dead, He can raise a dead church or ministry. With God, there is always hope.

While I was in Israel recently, I stood in the Valley of Elah. This is the famous place where David fought Goliath. You can clearly see two ridges where the opposing armies would have faced off against each other, and then a large valley in between. Goliath was a giant, 9 feet and 6 inches tall. He was intimidating and overwhelming. Yet, David was the only one of the Israelites brave enough to take him on. David said, "You come against me with a dagger, spear, and sword, but I come against you in the name of Yahweh of Hosts, the God of Israel's armies—you have defied Him" (1 Sam. 17:45). David won a great victory for Israel that day. Maybe you're facing some giants of your own. Like David, you will only win when you come against them in the name of the Lord.

You must be bold. Your faithfulness to God impacts more than just you. God wants to use you and your ministry to bless many. This is your time, so be strong in the Lord. Remember, it was churches that started schools, hospitals, orphanages, food pantries, hospices, and more. There were bold disciples of Jesus who went before us. Christians started schools like Harvard, Yale, and Penn, among others. Centers of higher learning. Now, some of these have drifted from their calling and mission over time, but they were started and used for years for the glory of God.

Every generation of Christ followers have had their day. Some ministered and started churches in the middle of wars, famines, and global pandemics. Maybe your parents, grandparents, or great-grandparents planted a church or started a nonprofit in their day. Praise God for their faithfulness. They have lifted up Jesus and made the world a better place.

And now it is our time. We have one opportunity—let's not miss it. Let's make the most of it, and let's be bold for the glory of God. Let's give our best for our Savior.

God is not finished with any of us yet. There is still breath in our lungs for a reason. Our best is still ahead of us, if we hold on to Jesus and stay true to His call in our lives.

God calls His people to serve. In church and in nonprofits, there are so many opportunities to make a difference in the lives of others. The amazing part, though, is how many times ours are the lives that are changed. Ministry is fueled by God's heart for the least, the lost, and the forgotten. We must always remember, as the Bible says, "if God is for us, who is against us?" (Rom. 8:31) When we know this and live this out, there is an incredible freedom that comes. My prayer for you is from 1 Corinthians 15:58, "Therefore, my dear brothers, be steadfast, immovable, always excelling in the Lord's work, knowing that your labor in the Lord is not in vain." Blessings on you and Godspeed as you build and invest in God's work and as you live out the business of ministry today.

ACKNOWLEDGMENTS

There are so many people to thank who helped make this book happen. I'm so grateful to my amazing Savior, who redeemed my life and has called me to lead and serve Him in a time such as this. In addition, I am so thankful for my amazing wife, Lisa, who has loved me and served alongside me in this journey. I love being married to her, raising our kids, and doing ministry together. I'm so grateful for our three amazing daughters, Grace, Mabry, and Kate, who love Jesus and serve Him so faithfully.

Along with Jesus and my family, I have so much love and appreciation for my church family at Rolling Hills Community Church. I love God's church, and I am so blessed to serve with the most amazing and godly servants of Christ Jesus. In addition, the staff of Justice & Mercy International in the US, the Amazon, and Moldova. What incredible, dedicated co-laborers in Christ.

Also, special thank you to Drew, Avrie, and the team at Moody Publishers who are so gifted, talented, and have been wonderful to work with on this book. Along those lines, thank you to my Administrative Professional, Jennifer Milligan, for helping make all this happen and keeping us on time, along with our Executive Pastor at Rolling Hills, Eric Rojas, and Mary Katharine Hunt, our Executive Director at JMI, who all personify the impact of business in ministry.

I am so blessed to be surrounded by such incredible brothers and sisters in Christ. I pray He will use this book to further His church in our day and generation. As you read this, know you are prayed for, and may you stay faithful to Him all the days of your life. Thanks for reading, and blessings on you, your family, and the ministry where you serve for the glory of our great God!

NOTES

1. Variations of this quotation exist; originally spoken in William Carey's sermon to the Baptist Association meeting in Nottingham, England, at the Friar Lane Baptist Chapel, May 30, 1792, www.wmcarey.edu/carey/expect/.

2. Mark Batterson, *Win the Day: 7 Daily Habits to Help You Stress Less & Accomplish More* (Colorado Springs: Multnomah, 2020), 107.

3. Rick Warren, "New Hope for Your Church Conference," Purpose Driven Conference (version 2.0), https://pastormentor.com/best-21-truths-learned-rick-warren/.

4. Eugene Peterson, "Introduction to Haggai," *The Message* (Colorado Springs: NavPress, 2007), 1300.

5. These words were recorded in a diary in 1863, quoting a Jesuit priest named Father Strickland; see "A Man May Do an Immense Deal of Good, If He Does Not Care Who Gets the Credit," Quote Investigator, December 21, 2010, https://quoteinvestigator.com/2010/12/21/doing-good-selfless/.

6. Lewis Carroll, *Alice in Wonderland* (1865; repr., The Floating Press, 2008), 50–51.

7. Andy Stanley, "Vision Leaks," *Christianity Today*, January 1, 2004, https://www.christianitytoday.com/pastors/2004/winter/andy-stanley-vision-leaks.html.

8. Les Brown, *Live Your Dreams* (New York: William Morrow and Company, 1992), 75.

9. Oswald Chambers, "The Key of the Greater Work," *My Utmost for His Highest*, https://utmost.org/the-key-of-the-greater-work/.

10. John Maxwell, *The 21 Irrefutable Laws of Leadership* (Nashville: Thomas Nelson, 2007), xi.

11. Charles H. Spurgeon, "Christ Manifesting Himself to His People," *New Park Street Pulpit Volume 1*, June 10, 1855, https://www.spurgeon.org/resource-library/sermons/christ-manifesting-himself-to-his-people/.

12. Rick Warren, *The Purpose Driven Life: What on Earth Am I Here For?* (Grand Rapids, MI: Zondervan, 2012), 149.

EVERYTHING THAT'S TAUGHT IN SEMINARY . . . ALL IN ONE PLACE!

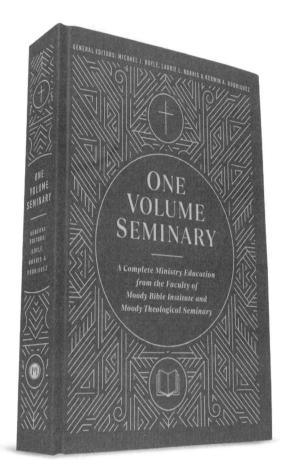